# Brave Together

## Devoted to God and Each Other

## Elisa Pulliam

Coach, Mentor, and Founder of MoreToBe.com

# Dedication

To all my sisters-in-Christ who have inspired me
to read the Word and apply it as we lived it out together.

*Is there any encouragement from belonging to Christ?*
*Any comfort from his love? Any fellowship together in the Spirit?*
*Are your hearts tender and compassionate?*
*Then make me truly happy by agreeing wholeheartedly*
*with each other, loving one another, and working together*
*with one mind and purpose.*

Philippians 2:1-2 NLT

# Table of Contents

# INTRODUCTION

## Becoming Brave Together

Do you long to become *the woman* God intended when He made you? The kind of woman who takes His Word and lives it out fully and bravely without compromise? The kind of woman who believes God's promises are true and His commands are tied to His blessings?

Maybe you've already been pursuing that kind of wholly devoted faith but ache for sisters to journey alongside you. Wouldn't it be nice to have at least one other woman who was as equally committed to living out God's Word? To seeing God transform every issue! To uncover the life of impact He designed!

You're not crazy or unrealistic to desire this type of fellowship steeped in faith. As a matter of fact, I'm certain that what you hope for is exactly what God wants to give you.

He wants you to have a fresh encounter with Himself and His Word. He wants you to live it out with other women who are in the trenches with you . . . women who are in your season and stage plus women who are older and younger than you. You were not meant to go through life alone, because you need exactly what your sisters-in-Christ can offer you as you seek to become the brave woman God intended.

How do I know this with such certainty? Because I wouldn't be who I am today without having been shaped by the godly women who have influenced every part of my life for the last 25 years.

God rescued me from a life of dysfunction and legacy of abuse, saving me by faith in Jesus Christ when I was a junior in college. For the next decade, I "tried" to be a Christian, conforming to the expectations of what real faith should look like. Don't get me wrong. I was sincere in my effort, but I lacked understanding in how to cultivate a brave and bold faith on my own.

 I didn't know how to read my Bible. I didn't know how to apply the Word. I didn't know how to get my issues with anger and insecurity under control. I didn't know what to do with my fears and worries and anxious thoughts. Praying didn't seem to be enough. Maybe you can relate?

I was floundering in my young faith but wasn't without hope. God plunked me down in a boarding school community where my husband worked and surrounded me with dozens of women, both at the boarding school and in my church, who unknowingly shaped my life. Those women inspired me, challenged me, sharpened me, and taught me about God's grace and love and His mercy and kindness.

---

**Yes, these were my brave sisters of God, from every generation and all walks of life, calling out the brave within me.**

---

Their small investment in my life through God-appointed conversations, Bible studies, and timely prayer groups reaped great dividends. Watching them in action as wives and mothers and devoted-to-the-Lord servants inspired me to seek my own fresh encounter with God and His Word . . . the kind of encounter that changed everything.

The closer I drew to the Lord, the braver I became in my faith. And the braver I became in my faith, the more I was able to trust God for the transformative work He was eager to accomplish in my life. Now, more than 25 years since I gave my life to Him, I can finally say I feel like I'm the woman He intended me to become. No, the work isn't done. We're continually growing in our faith, a genuine work progress, until we see Jesus face to face (Philippians 1:6). But oh my, it is such a joy to experience the kind of soul-deep, Spirit-led, courageous faith that He has given me now. I wholly believe He wants to give it to you too.

## You can become a woman of brave faith through experiencing a fresh encounter with God and His Word.

Yes, you can become brave in your faith and bold in your impact through pursuing more and more of God every day. As a life coach and mentor, I've had the opportunity to help women pursue God's best for their lives. That's what I want to do for you. You can take all that you are and all that you've experienced and lay it before God today and always, asking Him to redeem and resurrect your whole life for His glory.

You can yield to Him all your dreams and hopes, asking Him to align your heart's desires with His plan.

You can take the legacy you've come from and ask Him to lead you every step of the way in carving out a new one.

You can surrender all those habits and hang-ups that trap you in despair and ask Him to set you free with the truth.

You can be brave in all these ways and so many more. But you don't need to try to be brave alone.

## You need a community of brave sisters walking out this faith journey with you.

Yes, you need other women to speak into your life just like I had, so that they can show you the ropes you've yet to climb for yourself. I know that might prick a nerve, especially if you've been wounded by the women in your life. If that is your experience, I beg you to seek God's healing and extend forgiveness. It might feel hard on the front end, but sister it will be worth it in the long run.

## God didn't design for us to go at this life alone.

Acts 2 beautifully describes what a community of believers ought to enjoy together: devotion to the teaching of God's Word, fellowship, and prayer.

*The Believers Form a Community*
*All the believers devoted themselves to the apostles' teaching, and*
*to fellowship, and to sharing in meals (including the Lord's Supper),*
*and to prayer.*
ACTS 2:42 NLT

Certainly, this is the ideal for our church community, but isn't it also a perfect model for creating a *Brave Together* community of women around us? The problem, at least in America, is our busyness, work commitments, and family responsibilities. But just because it's hard doesn't mean we should give up on the call to connect with other believers. I can hear your excuses and fears taking over. *But do I really need others?* Yes, you do! First Corinthians 12 describes the importance of believers being connected to one another.

*All of you together are Christ's body,*
*and each of you is a part of it.*
1 CORINTHIANS 12:27 NLT

We are designed to be a part of the body of Christ. Each one of us serves a need. Each one of us must meet a need, as we all have weaknesses and strengths. So who is in the body right next to you that you can reach out to without it being overly complicated to connect? Who are those older Christ-following women God has placed in your life? Who is in the trenches with you? Who is coming up behind you? Don't just look in your church. Look also in your workplace. Your neighborhood. And even connections with friends spread across the globe who you can connect with over Skype or Voxer (an App for your phone).

Now imagine linking arms with them as you pursue God purposefully for real-life change and legacy-leaving impact. Imagine making a commitment together to cultivate deeper relationships with one another around the common mission of living out the Word daily. No, you don't have to be in the same place to spur each other on towards spiritual growth. You just have to be invested in the process and willing to be creative in your approach. That's where *Brave Together* comes in.

---

### *Brave Together* **is a tool for building a meaningful community of sisters devoted to growing in their faith together.**

---

Within *Brave Together*, you'll find 52 different biblical principles designed to help you live out a brave, bold, bright, and beautiful faith. These principles are connected with a life-application devotional plus a Scripture prayer and application question. With this three-pillar approach — Connect {with God}, Consider {the Word}, Cultivate {your Faith} — you have the opportunity to not only grow personally but also cultivate biblical mentoring relationships by using the content as a conversation starter within your *Brave Together* community.

Sure, you can read through *Brave Together* on your own. But how much more meaningful would it be to spend an entire year committed to spiritual growth with other women who share your passion for becoming more and more like the woman God always intended? Trust me, when you see God at work in each other, you'll be all the more motivated to keep on pressing on. That kind of motivation will not only lead you to experience real transformation through a fresh encounter with God and His Word but will also result in you becoming the kind of woman who impacts this world and especially the next generation with Kingdom hope.

> *Is there any encouragement from belonging to Christ?*
> *Any comfort from his love? Any fellowship together in the Spirit?*
> *Are your hearts tender and compassionate?*
> *Then make me truly happy by agreeing wholeheartedly*
> *with each other, loving one another, and working together*
> *with one mind and purpose.*
> PHILIPPIANS 2:1-2 NLT

So, will you take the next step and be the one who starts a *Brave Together* community of sisters devoted to living out His Word together?

# How to Use

This book is built upon the *Brave Women Manifesto,* which is a collection of 52 biblical principles that remind us how to think biblically and live transformed. Within each chapter, you'll find:

- Brave Manifesto Principle
- Key Verses and Recommended Readings
- **Connect {with God}:** Scripture prayer to help you connect with God
- **Consider {the Word}:** Devotional with biblical application principle
- **Cultivate {your Faith}:** Application question and challenge

While *Brave Together* is wonderful for personal study, the vision is for you to use it with other women of all ages, stages, and seasons of life. Consider these possibilities:

### Create a *Brave Together* Accountability Group

Invite one or more women to join you in reading *Brave Together* over the course of the year. Commit to a weekly check-in with each other over text, email, a Facebook group, Voxer (app for your phone) group, or in person, using the application question to share your thoughts with one another.

### Pursue a *Brave Together* Mentoring Relationship

Invite a younger or older woman to commit to a six to twelve month mentoring relationship using the principles found in *Impact Together: Biblical Mentoring Simplified* (available at MoretoBe.com and Amazon) and use *Brave Together* for your meeting time discussions.

### Host a *Brave Together* Monthly Gathering

Gather a group of women or tween/teen/college age girls together for a monthly *Brave Together* Gathering and pick a couple of the devotions to discuss.

**Lead a *Brave Together* Bible Study**

Invite a group to join you for a more in-depth Bible study using a selection of the devotions to go deeper into the word for four to eight weeks at a time.

**Use *Brave Together* as a Conversation Starter**

Pick the individual devotions to start a conversation with your tween, teen, or college-age daughter to address a topic you would like to share from a biblical perspective.

However you choose to use *Brave Together*, I pray that God will lead, guide, and equip you. You have the opportunity before you to experience God at work in you and through you as you seek Him purposefully.

# The Brave Women Manifesto

So let us come boldly to the
throne of our gracious God.
There we will receive his mercy,
and we will find grace to help
us when we need it most.

Hebrews 4:16

1.  I will not accept "as is" as a way of life because God is not yet done with the work He began in me and intends to use my life in His good work. (Philippians 1:6; Ephesians 2:10)

2.  I will acknowledge that I have been bought at a price for my sin, for which Jesus Christ died on the cross so that I might be made right before God. (Romans 3:22-28)

3.  I will love the Lord my God with all my heart, my soul, my mind. (Deuteronomy 6:5; Matthew 22:37)

4.  I will trust in the Lord my God with all my heart and seek His purposes for my life. (Psalm 28:7; Proverbs 3:5-6)

5.  I will humbly and boldly share the truth that all have sinned and fallen short of the glory of God, but that God made a way for all to be saved through Jesus Christ. (Romans 3:23; John 3:16)

6.  I will take captive my thoughts and make them obedient to Christ. (2 Corinthians 10:5)

7.  I will allow God to transform my life through renewing my mind in the Word each day. (Romans 12:2)

8.  I will confess my sin before God daily before bringing my requests before Him. (Hosea 14:2; Psalm 5:3, 66:18)

9.  I will fix my thoughts on whatever is true, and honorable, and right, and pure, and lovely, and admirable, and excellent, and praiseworthy. (Philippians 4:8)

10. I will choose to be kind and speak kind words to others. (Ephesians 4:32; Proverbs 16:24)

11. I will be honest about my issues with God and seek His help (and counseling when needed) for overcoming sin, strongholds, and addictions. (Psalm 51; Romans 12:3)

12. I will be the first to say I'm sorry, seek forgiveness, and offer forgiveness even when it's hard. (Psalm 38:18; James 5:16; Luke 17:4)

13. I will remember that I am fearfully and wonderfully made, not on accident, but on purpose for a good purpose. (Psalm 139; Ephesians 2:10)

14. I will commit to accountability relationships with one to two other women. (2 Timothy 2:22)

15. I will make it a habit to speak in psalms, hymns, and spiritual songs. (Colossians 3:16)

16. I will strive to do everything for the glory of God. (1 Corinthians 10:31)

17. I will be a woman of my word. (Matthew 5:37)

18. I will seek God for a changed heart before trying to change my circumstances. (Ezekiel 36:26)

19. I will guard my heart by considering what I expose myself to each day. (Proverbs 4:23)

20. I will pursue a life of whole-heart, whole-mind, whole-body purity. (Psalm 86:11; Hebrews 13:4)

21. I will carefully consider the words I choose to speak. (Matthew 12:37, 15:11, 18)

22. I will watch my words to consider the state of my heart. (Proverbs 15:28; Luke 6:45)

23. I will do all I can to live in peace with others. (Romans 12:18)

24. I will remember that my life is a story God is writing for others to see Him. (2 Corinthians 3:3)

25. I will love others without fear of rejection as His love overflows through me. (1 Thessalonians 3:12; 2 Timothy 1:7; 1 John 4:18)

26. I will fear God and not seek the approval of any man or woman. (Psalm 34:9; Matthew 10:28; Philippians 2:12; Galatians 1:10)

27. I will be thankful to God in all circumstances. (1 Thessalonians 5:18)

28. I will be teachable and seek wisdom from godly counsel. (Proverbs 2:2, 15:31; James 1:5)

29. I will honor others because they are made in the image of God. (Genesis 1:27; Romans 12:10)

30. I will respect the men in my life and not belittle or degrade them. (Ephesians 5:33; 1 Timothy 5:1)

31. I will not make an idol of anyone (especially spouse or children) or anything (project, title, degree, accomplishment). (Deuteronomy 4:23)

32. I will continue to ask God to enable me to live a life worthy of His call with the power to accomplish all things as my faith prompts me to do. (2 Thessalonians 1:11)

33. I will seek God daily for a deeper understanding of His Word as

truth. (John 17:17; Hebrews 4:12)

34. I will strive to be filled up by Jesus Christ, the Living Water, and not others. (John 4:10, 7:38)

35. I will remember that God gives life to the full, the abundant life, but the enemy comes to steal, kill, and destroy. (John 10:10)

36. I will learn to sit quietly to hear from God. (Psalm 46:10)

37. I will devote time to pray for those God has brought into my life and the needs He lays on my heart. (Matthew 26:41; 1 Thessalonians 3:10, 5:17)

38. I will not forsake a commitment to a church body, even when it is hard. (Hebrews 10:25)

39. I will use my gifts to serve the body of Christ for the glory of God. (1 Corinthians 12; Romans 12:3-8)

40. I will allow God's power to be made perfect in my weaknesses. (2 Corinthians 12:19)

41. I will make the most of every opportunity the Lord gives me. (Ephesians 5:16)

42. I will seek God to fill me with all joy and peace as I trust in Him that I may overflow with hope onto others by the power of the Holy Spirit at work in me. (Romans 15:13)

43. I will yield my financial resources to the Lord's work. (Malachi 3:8-10; Mark 12:41-44)

44. I will seek justice, love mercy, and walk humbly all of my days.

(Micah 6:8)

45. I will defend the cause of the fatherless, the poor, the oppressed. (Psalm 82:3)

46. I will speak the Good News and live out the Gospel in private and public. (Psalm 40:10; Matthew 24:14)

47. I will accept the trouble and suffering that comes into my life, knowing that God will equip me to endure and be my comforter. (Matthew 6:34; 2 Corinthians 1:3,7; 2 Corinthians 4:8-10)

48. I will always choose to believe that God is indeed holy, kind, loving, faithful, merciful, and just. (Romans 2:4; Lamentations 3:22-23; Psalm 36:5)

49. I will strive to lay down my life for others as Christ has done for me. (John 15:13)

50. I will obey God because I love God. (1 John 2:5)

51. I will put on the full armor of God as I fight against the enemy of God and not the people of God. (Ephesians 6:10-19)

52. I will seek to live as a chosen, holy, dearly loved child of God who has been called out of darkness and into His wonderful light, that I may tell others about His marvelous works and praise His holy name. (Colossians 3:12; 1 Peter 2:9)

*If you would like a printable version of this manifesto, visit moretobe.com/brave-together/*

# 1

I will not accept "as is" as a way of life, because God is not yet done with the work He began in me and intends to use my life in His good work.

*... being confident of this, that he who began a good work in you will carry it on to completion until the day of Christ Jesus.*
PHILIPPIANS 1:6

*For we are God's handiwork, created in Christ Jesus to do good works, which God prepared in advance for us to do.*
EPHESIANS 2:10

# Connect

Heavenly Father, thank you for the good work You began in us long before we ever considered joining You in Your work.

---

**Thank you for the ways You have manifested Your purposes in our lives, even at times when we have felt alone and defeated.**

---

Thank you that Your work is not limited to our abilities, but transforms our gifts and talents in ways that are only possible through the infusing of Your Holy Spirit within us.

Lord, please forgive us when we get in the way of Your work, when we yield to our flesh and become consumed by our own desires. Forgive us for the junk we hold onto in our hearts and minds, that crowds out Your presence and the way You want to work in our lives.

Help us, Lord, to see Your purposes. Help us to embrace Your plans. Give us eyes to see how You're transforming our "as is" life into something remarkably beautiful from an eternal perspective.

In the strong name of Jesus, Amen.

# Consider

If you took a tour of my home, you'd find that there is a story in nearly every piece of furniture. Their "as is" condition reveals a long journey before they came to us as a hand-me-down, road-side find, or were uncovered in the far corners of a discount store.

While it's awesome to furnish your home at a fraction of the retail cost, there's another aspect of picking up "as is" furniture that's priceless—it's the memories that are made in the acquisition.

Like that time I was heading out with the girls and we passed this beautiful but monstrous armoire on the side of the road. We circled back around two times, bantering about whether it would fit in our van, but never questioning whether we could lift the thing in the first place. I finally gave in to the girls' enthusiasm, and we pulled up right in front the beauty, put the van seats down, tipped the giant backwards, and tried to shove it into the back. We were about ready to give up, realizing we had misjudged the girth of the piece, when a man from across the street started walking toward us. We panicked that he wanted it, but instead he said, "Ladies, would you like some help? I can drive it to your house in the back of my pickup truck."

If you could have heard the squeals of my HGTV enamored tween girls. They thought we had hit the jackpot, and that's exactly how they tell the story every time someone admires the piece in our home … the most imperfect piece with sticky drawers and cabinet doors that don't stay shut.

Oh yes, it is "as is," but that's what makes it special. It tells a story of a life lived before it came to us and reminds us of a crazy moment when the kindness of a stranger was an unexpected blessing. I can't help but think that God looks at us the same way.

---

## We are His creation, marred by sin, but made fearfully and wonderfully with a good purpose.

---

We may feel "as is," but the Lord is capable of using us as we are and redeeming even the most broken parts for His glorious purposes … telling a story of His work.

## Cultivate

Do you feel like you're "as is"? If so, what might God want to do with you in a redeemed condition?

# 2

I will acknowledge that I have been bought at a price for my sin, for which Jesus Christ died on the cross, so that I might be made right before God.

*We are made right with God by placing our faith in Jesus Christ. And this is true for everyone who believes, no matter who we are. For everyone has sinned; we all fall short of God's glorious standard. Yet God, in his grace, freely makes us right in his sight. He did this through Christ Jesus when he freed us from the penalty for our sins. For God presented Jesus as the sacrifice for sin.*
ROMANS 3:22-25

# Connect

Heavenly Father, thank you for Your amazing and glorious grace. Thank you for making a way for us to be in a right relationship with You through placing our faith in Your Son, Jesus Christ, as our Savior.

Oh God, thank you for ordaining it that Your Son's death on the cross would free us from the penalty of sin. Lord, forgive us when we try to earn Your love ... a love that You have already given to us through the shedding of Christ's blood on the cross on our behalf. Thank you for not punishing us as our sins ... as our wrong doings and disobedience ... deserve.

---

## Thank you, God, for being fair and just.

---

Thank you that we are already accepted by You, God, because of our faith in Jesus Christ. Lord, may we live out this truth boldly and bravely this week, choosing to no longer live in fear and in doubt of Your acceptance of us. May we walk in courageous confidence, knowing that we are already accepted and dearly loved by You.

May Your love and truth overflow onto those around us, thus making a relationship with You attractive in their eyes. May the people in our lives know that You are for them, as they see how You're for us.

In the strong name of Jesus, Amen.

# *Consider*

Not long after we bought our first home, we discovered that the promise of a home warranty wasn't nearly as great as we hoped. While we anticipated some immediate repairs, like the roof and fridge, we were in no way prepared to replace the boiler. Both the inspector and former homeowner never indicated there was any problem, even though we realized after it was too late that the leak between the chambers of the aging unit was the source of the water stain on the floor.

We were duped, not only by what we didn't know to look for, but also by the fine print.

The promise of a home warranty led us to believe that should the boiler fail within a year of purchase, we'd have the whole replacement covered. Ah. Not so. See, the fine print in that warranty said, "Up to $1,500." Do you know how much it costs to replace a boiler system? I hope you're sitting down, because ours cost more than $8,000, and that was not the most expensive quote.

As I reflect upon how unprepared we were to be homeowners, and the financial strain of owning a house, it often makes me think of God and the promise of salvation. I know that may seem odd, but stick with me for a minute.

---

## When it comes to God and His Word, there is no hidden fine print.

---

His Word, when it is revealed to us by the Holy Spirit, is plain and straightforward. We may not understand His ways, but we can count on God to always be faithful, always be true. He is never changing and full of loving kindness, always.

Unlike owning a house, and not knowing what it will really cost to maintain it until you're in the thick of it, God takes care of all the charges when we choose to enter into a relationship with Him.

God doesn't ever expect more of us than we have to give.

He bought us at a price … through the death of His Son, Jesus Christ … and makes a way for us to be right with Him. To us, this is a free gift. To God, it cost Him everything.

With owning a house, there's always this sense of "Oh no, what's going to break next … and what will it cost us?" But with God, there is the promise of eternity, no matter what the earthly strain might be.

In Christ, however, we have full confidence that the price of eternity has been secured for us.

## Cultivate

How does the fact that God reveals everything we need to know in the Word, and through the working of the Holy Spirit, change how we face our circumstances today?

# 3

I will love the Lord my God with all my heart, my soul, my mind.

*And you must love the Lord your God with all your heart, all your soul, and all your strength.*
DEUTERONOMY 6:5

*Jesus replied, "'You must love the Lord your God with all your heart, all your soul, and all your mind.'"*
MATTHEW 22:37

# Connect

Heavenly Father, twice You give us such a simple command ... to love You ... with all our heart, soul, and mind. And yet we fail. Miserably. Often. Unintentionally. Carelessly. Maybe, sometimes on purpose. We fail to love You with everything within our being.

Please, God, forgive us. Forgive us for the way we so easily toss our love toward things and people and pursuits that won't care for it like You do, won't return it like You do, won't nurture it like You do. Forgive us for holding back from loving You with everything in our heart, with all our soul, with every bit of our mind.

God, You knew this love command would be hard for us, but You didn't let it slide by. You had Jesus bring it front and center, because it's that important to You. Lord, if Your number one call on our lives is to love You, then make that our number one desire.

---

**Please help us eradicate from our lives the distractions that steal our love.**

---

Help us demolish false gods and crush every bit of idolatry that sneaks in and steals our heart, soul, and mind. Enable us to love You with a pure heart with every shred of our being. May that be our holy pursuit with each and every breath.

In the strong name of Jesus, Amen.

## Consider

Being brave women is about being as real as we can get, even if that means we have to get uncomfortably honest and 'fess up our issues. I've said it for years, I think we all need T-shirts that say, "I've got issues. . . but God isn't done with me yet." So, how about if we start by me sharing my issues as it relates to this command from God to love Him with all our heart, soul, and mind?

Loving God is not something that came naturally to me. As a child of abuse, I had a warped understanding of love. In searching for it, I became a people-pleasing, approval-addicted teen and twenty-something, who was pretty good at destroying relationships before they could destroy me. Ah, yes, I was emotionally and spiritually unhealthy, even after coming to know Christ as my Savior during my junior year in college.

It wasn't until years later that I realized the depth of my wounding and dysfunction and how it warped my understanding of God as a loving, heavenly Father. Through a good bit of counseling, a whole lot of prayer, and a deep study of Scripture, the Lord opened my eyes to see God afresh. I eventually realized that God's commands were meant for our good—both the commands that call us away from hurtful behavior and those, like the ones found in Deuteronomy 6 and Matthew 22, that call us into heart-soul-and-mind healthy living.

---

**When God urges us to love Him with all our being, He's inviting us to let go of everything toxic.**

---

Even though I knew that people wouldn't ever satisfy my soul, I'd yet to discover how to receive God's love and return it in full measure. He had a part of my heart, where my faith dwelled, but not the part still searching for approval. I was caught in the stronghold of idolatry throughout my thirties, making idols of my accomplishments and titles and ministry and projects. But by the grace of God, He opened my eyes to see that my worth would never be found in anything but Him, and His love was not dependent on all my "doings."

---

## God can love us no more or no less than He already does.

---

Once I embraced that truth, a love for God began to fill my heart and soul and mind in a way I never before experienced, as a new way of thinking took over. You are so loved by God, so just love Him back.

Even so, I'm still learning how to love God. The habit of loving everything else more isn't one that dies easily. But I'm motivated by the fact that when I love someone or something more than God, I'm not only forsaking the command He's put before us to love Him with all our heart, soul, and mind, but I'm also walking in disobedience, even if it is unintentional. That's a harsh reality, isn't it? And that's not how I want to live. What about you?

## Cultivate

How is God calling you to live for Him with all your heart, soul, and mind? How does His love for you shape that call?

# 4

I will trust in the Lord my God with all my heart and seek His purposes for my life.

*The Lord is my strength and my shield;*
*my heart trusts in him, and he helps me.*
*My heart leaps for joy,*
*and with my song I praise him.*
PSALM 28:7

*Trust in the Lord with all your heart*
*and lean not on your own understanding;*
*in all your ways submit to him,*
*and he will make your paths straight.*
PROVERBS 3:5-6

# *Connect*

Lord, we are so grateful that You promise to be our strength and our shield. God, we want our hearts to leap for joy at the thought of You. And yet, we know there are secret places tucked away in our hearts, in which we store up parts of our lives that we think are untouchable by You, because we're afraid about what You'll do with those parts, if we give You access.

Lord, why do we feel this way when You are indeed trustworthy? Is it because we're looking at You through wounded eyes? Is it because we think you'll fail us, shame us, and hurt us the way we've experienced in our flesh?

---

## Oh God, forgive me for not believing You are who You say You are.

---

Fill our heart and mind with increasing trust in Your character as a faithful, loving, just, and merciful God who wants good for His daughter. Fill our hearts with a song of praise to You, Oh Lord. Fill us with joy, Father, as we trust in You more.

Remind us to not lean on our own understanding, but instead, give all our thoughts and hopes and dreams to You. To give our plans to You … moment by moment.

God, I ask You to make our paths straight. Work yourself more fully into our hearts, minds, and souls, that we may sense Your presence, hear Your voice, and heed Your leading in every area of our lives.

In the strong name of Jesus, Amen.

# Consider

Trusting God isn't my natural tendency, especially as a big idea girl with lots of plans for the future swirling in my head. Nonetheless, I haven't been able to escape this clear instruction from God to trust Him with all my heart. From the time my girls entered kindergarten, we recited Proverbs 3:5, 6 again and again, as it was their elementary school's theme verse.

Trusting God has never felt more real than now, as my once little kindergartner rounds the corner of her last semester of her senior year of high school. Bless her precious planning heart, as she's just like her mama and desperately wants to know what's next. Yet in this season in her life, it's all about the not knowing.

---

**It's about the waiting and learning to more fully trust God with all!**

---

She's waiting on college acceptances, rejections, and financial aid packages yet to be determined. She's eager to eliminate possibilities and clarify the direction of her life, but the reality is that even those earthly predictors of her future can't begin to reveal God's straight path ahead. He can turn her circumstances at a moment's notice and throw a curve ball whenever He likes, just as He did in relocating us right before her junior year in high school.

Her bucket list dreams were dashed in a tumultuous upheaval. And yet, that was God's straight path for her … one in which she had to learn to trust Him more.

My girl is not the only one having to put her trust in God. I am most certainly overwhelmed by the ending of a long-lived season. Where's my little girl? How did she grow up so fast? What can I do to slow down time and keep her under my wing? Is she really ready to fly? Can I really trust God will all my heart, believing that He can care for her better than I?

And so, together, as mother and daughter becoming co-equal sisters in Christ, we are learning to walk in deeper faith. We are learning to trust Him more.

## Cultivate

How can you yield your life to His purposes, not only for yourself, but those you love?

# 5

I will humbly and boldly share
the truth that all have sinned
and fallen short of the glory of God,
but that God made a way for all
to be saved through Jesus Christ.

*... for all have sinned and fall short of the glory of God ...*
ROMANS 3:23

*For God so loved the world that he gave his one and only Son,
that whoever believes in him shall not perish but have eternal life.*
JOHN 3:16

# Connect

Oh God, this matter of sin is simply uncomfortable and often offensive, especially for those who don't know how loving, kind, and gracious You are to us. All too often it feels like we're casting a judgment, to point out the fact that we're all sinners, rather than revealing the amazing extravagant gift You gave us in Christ.

---

**God, in our world where sacrifice is a dirty word and selfishness is the norm, the cross is incomprehensible unless You open the eyes of the blind.**

---

So do we even need to talk about it? Can't we just pray for others to see You and recognize how their sinfulness is a desperate cry for a Savior? Oh God, forgive us for our lack of courage. Please make us braver to share the truth and point to Jesus.

Forgive us, God, for not calling sin as it is and instead softening the blow with "I just messed up." Oh, how could we be more wrong? To mess up means we had a chance to do it right in the first place.

Forgive us, God, for making much of our mess and so little of the sacrifice our sin cost You.

Forgive us, God, for even trying to be good enough! As sinners, we won't ever be righteous enough!

You love us so much that You accept us as we are, but You don't leave us that way. Isn't that why You sent Your Son to die on the cross for the forgiveness of our sins? Help us to not make light of Jesus' blood, which was sacrificed to satisfy the debt of our sin.

In the strong name of Jesus, Amen.

# *Consider*

Ah, sin. I hate it. Who doesn't? And yet, our hatred of sin doesn't keep us from sinning. Maybe it deters us from a sinful course a time or two, but it doesn't eradicate it from our lives. That's because being sinful is inherent to who we are.

While God created us perfect, His perfect creation didn't obey His commands.

As my youngest is most vocal about expressing, "Why did Adam and Eve have to disobey God in the Garden of Eden and bring sin into this world?" Yep, our wayward course can be traced back to the very beginning.

In our family, you'll find us often talking about sin, because I've been bent on dealing with mine for a long, long time. I'll be the first to admit that my sin, manifested in anger issues, could have wrecked my family, along with years of stored up bitterness and unforgiveness. But owning my mess before God and yielding to His work in my heart has truly transformed me from the inside out. It hasn't made me perfect or sinless, but it has made me want to shine the light in the darkness of sin and see God set us FREER today than we were yesterday.

---

## Without Jesus, our mess stays messy.

---

But with Jesus, our mess is called out as sin, and that sin has been paid for by His blood shed on the cross. Jesus wasn't just about providing us with salvation. He's also all about our sanctification. Being saved might be a once-and-done experience, but being sanctified is God's lifetime work in our lives. That sanctification manifests in an honest, humble, and holy relationship with God, where we call our "messes" sin and quickly seek His forgiveness. It doesn't matter if it's the kind of public sin that all can see, like lashing out in anger, or the private kind in which pride oozes from the heart unnoticed by those closest to us. It doesn't matter if it's the kind of sin that is kept in secret for a decade or the type that is like a firework going off that quickly dissipates into thin air.

Sin is pervasive. As Eugene Peterson says, "Every congregation is a congregation of sinners. As if that weren't bad enough, they all have sinners for pastors."

Yes, all have sinned and fallen short of the glory of God. Every one of us can echo Paul's words in 1 Timothy 1:15, "Christ Jesus came into the world to save sinners—and I am the worst of them all."

We all need Jesus to save us from our sin.

## Cultivate

What does it look like for us to keep short accounts with God and be quick to own our sin?

# 6

I will take captive my thoughts
and make them obedient to Christ.

*[Inasmuch as we] refute arguments and theories and reasonings
and every proud and lofty thing that sets itself up against the [true]
knowledge of God; and we lead every thought and purpose away
captive into the obedience of Christ (the Messiah, the Anointed One).*
2 CORINTHIANS 10:5 AMP

# *Connect*

Lord God, it is so true that the battle for our lives begins in our minds. It's in our thought life that we give way to our actions. Isn't that why You urge us to do more than just take notice of our thoughts? You want us to take action and be cautious about what we choose to dwell upon in our minds, because that's where actions begin to form.

Oh Lord, this principle is so simple. So profound. So necessary. And yet, we ignore it all too often. We let our thoughts wander here and there, to and fro, without considering the consequence. We expose our minds to input that is unholy and wholly destructive. Maybe it doesn't feel that way at first, but it always ends up there. We allow ourselves too much time to muse upon our feelings, instead of telling our feelings to fall in line with the truth. We speak out loud words of falsehood, so often from a place of wounding, instead of soaking in Your wisdom and proclaiming the hope of Your healing.

---

**Forgive us, God. Change us, God.
Make our thought life obedient to Christ.**

---

God, give us a holy boldness to do battle in our minds so that we may be wholly submitted to You. Give us the courage to let go of the lies we've always believed and embrace the truth You have given us in Your Word. God, give us honest words filled with grace and truth to speak over ourselves and to those You've placed in our lives.

In the strong name of Jesus, Amen.

# Consider

For the last decade, I've been actively demolishing the lies sown into my heart and mind. It has been like removing wallpaper, ripping down one sheet at a time. Sometimes the process is long and tedious, only to expose another layer of lies, sown into my heart decades ago. Lies, like …

*You're so stupid. When God was handing out brains, you thought He said trains, and didn't get in line.*

*You'll never be able to get along with anyone.*

*You can't trust anyone—they will always cheat, leave, and reject you.*

Left unchecked, these lies have the power to dominate my thinking and impact my living.

---

**Did you know that a child's worldview and belief system is shaped by the time they are six years old? If it is left unchallenged, it can stay with them for a lifetime.**

---

By God's grace, my belief system was challenged and continued to be pressed in upon with the truth of God's Word through the love of my husband, mentors, and dear friends. I wish it were a once-and-done process, but as I shared in *Meet the New You* when I describe the Trap & Transform process that the book is built upon, trapping our thoughts and being transformed by God through renewing our minds with the truth is a daily process.

Using our "powerful God-tools for smashing warped philosophies, tearing down barriers erected against the truth of God, fitting every loose thought and emotion and impulse into the structure of life shaped by Christ," we can take the lies captive with the truth. Those lies ingrained in my mind now have the potential of a new thought pattern …

> *You're not stupid. You are fearfully and wonderfully made. (Psalm 139)*

> *You might not get along with everyone, because it requires effort to live in peace with everyone. (Romans 12:18)*

> *You may be betrayed by humankind, because all have sinned and fallen short of the glory of God. But in Christ we find forgiveness, healing, and redemption. God is trustworthy. (Romans 3:23; Matthew 6:14; Romans 4:7)*

Isn't it time for you to engage in this battle for truth … a battle for your mind, heart, soul, and Christ-centered identity?

# Cultivate

What is one lie you can replace with the truth today?

# 1

I will allow God to transform my
life through renewing my mind
in the Word each day.

*Don't copy the behavior and customs of this world,*
*but let God transform you into a new person by changing*
*the way you think. Then you will learn to know God's will*
*for you, which is good and pleasing and perfect.*

ROMANS 12:2

# *Connect*

Father God, there isn't a single one of us who doesn't long for some sort of transformation. Oh Lord, we may be too prideful to admit it … or too fearful to face it … but the reality is that we'll never become who You intended on this side of heaven without Your transformation work taking place inside our minds.

---

## God, please transform our hang-ups, hold-ups, and unhealthy habits into holiness.

---

Yet, Lord, how often we take our issues and turn to the world for solutions. We chase after a quick fix and pain-free disguises, but never get to the root of the issue. Only in desperation do we seek You out, wishing You'd solve our problems without inconveniencing us.

Forgive us, God, for not turning to You first.

It really is so simple, Lord. You just want us to give You access to our heart and mind. You want us to get into the Word daily so that You can change the way we think. Oh Lord, why do we resist spending time reading Your love letter to us?

Make us hungry for Your Word. Make our appetites voracious for chewing on Your truth. Make us unable to find satisfaction for our souls any other way.

Protect us from the temptation to turn elsewhere. Protect us from distraction. Protect us from the hollow philosophies of this world. Give us a deep, soulful longing for Your pleasing and perfect will above all things.

In the strong name of Jesus, Amen.

# Consider

Imagine if I were sitting across the table from you at my favorite local coffee shop, slowly sipping a perfectly made cappuccino while confessing to you my struggle to keep my plate balanced. On the outside, you can't imagine that would be the case. I look the part of a perfectly put together woman. But don't let appearances fool you.

It was a scramble to even show up on time, as I used up every last second to respond to e-mails, edit a final post, double check comments, and send an invoice. That's just the work crazies. Wander around my home and you'd find the sink piled up with dishes because we forgot to run the load the night before. The living room rug looks like our Golden Retriever spent at least a week rolling all over it, when I vacuumed only a day ago. Laundry is beckoning to be folded and put away, and the garage, which is not my domain, looks like an obstacle course of tools, recycling, and building projects that I inspired.

So there I sit across from you, lamenting about my sense of chaos. I confess I feel like a mess. I know I'm giving it my all, but is it good enough? I know a perfectly kept home is not something my family nor God expects of me, so why do I feel so bad about it? I know I'm doing what God has called me to and my husband and children support me, but ... can I do it all better? What would you say in response?

Would you be tempted to agree with me about my shortcomings? Would you share you own woes to try to make me feel better? Would you feel irritated that I had the nerve to complain, compared to what you're going through now?

I only ask because as I was reflecting on this Brave Manifesto principle, something struck me afresh, thanks to my perspective as a life coach in the throws of teaching a coach certification class four times a week. The fact is that your empathy, storytelling, or advice-giving won't solve my problem. Joining in my pity party might be a tender way to acknowledge that the struggle is real, but that won't fix it either. So what is the best way to respond?

What if our response went something like this …

*Oh friend, I hear your struggle. But may I ask you a few tough questions, because I really do care for you and what you're feeling? Have you brought this struggle before the Lord?*
Um. Sort of.

*So what do you hear Him saying to you?*
Well, I need to breathe and not be so hard on myself.

*Ah, yes. That is good. What else is He saying to you?*
Honestly, I've felt this conviction that I need to stop rushing through my Bible study homework, just to get it done, and I need to linger longer in the Word.

*So, what would happen if you heeded that conviction?*
I know when I start the day with my whole heart and mind focused on God and in His Word it changes how I approach what's coming at me. When I pray, "Lord, please order the details of my day," it shifts how I look at my time and priorities.

*Wow, so what can I do to encourage you to begin your day in the Word with that kind of focus, and not just a checklist mentality?*

Imagine how much more beneficial this type of conversation between sisters in Christ would be as opposed to the usual sorrowful-story swap we tend to fall into.

---

**I know it's not easy to patiently ask the obvious questions, but friend, it works.**

---

This is exactly what I teach to the women in my life coach training course. Imagine the impact of using this skill among friends willing to "call each other out" in areas of spiritual growth! Friend, isn't this what brave faith is all about ... growing together as we become the women God intended?

## Cultivate

How can you encourage your sisters-in-Christ to dig deep in the Word and cultivate friendships that challenge you to do the same?

# 8

I will confess my sin before God daily before bringing my requests before Him.

*Bring your confessions, and return to the Lord.*
*Say to him, "Forgive all our sins and graciously*
*receive us, so that we may offer you our praises."*
HOSEA 14:2

*Listen to my voice in the morning, Lord. Each morning*
*I bring my requests to you and wait expectantly.*
PSALM 5:3

*If I had not confessed the sin in my heart,*
*the Lord would not have listened.*
PSALM 66:18

# Connect

Heavenly Father, thank you for the invitation to come to You daily and for giving us a pattern to follow … to rise in the morning and speak with You right away. Forgive us, Lord, when we turn elsewhere first.

It's so hard, Lord, to push off the demands and distractions to make time to sit with You. We have this idea in our minds about what a "perfect time" together should look like, and the enemy most certainly uses it to defeat us. Rather than giving our best, we give You nothing at all, feeling as though what we can offer is not good enough.

---

**Oh Lord, break us free from this bondage of unrealistic expectations and perfect pursuits.**

---

God, please remind us that this invitation to come to You is rooted in love with no strings attached. Remind us of Your kindness and gentleness. Remind us that confessing our sins before You is a GREAT thing to do, because You forgive us.

Thank you for pouring out Your new mercies every morning. Please, Lord, impress this on our hearts so that we can live brave and bold, bright and beautiful, totally unhindered by sin that so easily entangles us.

Set us free, God, with Your forgiveness.

In the strong name of Jesus, Amen.

# *Consider*

Does the idea of confessing your sin make you squirm? Would you rather push it to the back burner a bit and deal with it later? Or does this topic of sin bring to mind a laundry list of mistakes, mishaps, shortcomings, and downright disobedience? Do you feel like your life has been nothing short of one sin-stained fiasco after another?

Well, the good news is this: God doesn't categorize our sin the way we do.

But He doesn't look the other way either. He sees our sin plainly. He sees our brokenness clearly. He sees our guilt before we've even identified it for ourselves.

---

## The God of the universe decided in advance what to do with all that He sees and knows.

---

While we're tap dancing around "the issue," He's not. He knows sin erects a wall between us, and so He's made a way for it to be torn down. Why? Because we are His children and He desires to be intimately connected to us ... a connection that can't happen as long as we're actively sinning.

God ordained that Jesus' death on the cross satisfies the debt for our sin once and for all.

While Christ's shed blood doesn't remove the consequences we might experience, we do not need to live apart from an intimate relationship with God ... no matter what sin we've committed.

In His kindness, God invites us to keep clean accounts with Him. He waits patiently for us to speak our first breath to His bent ear.

God, in His remarkable, holy, and compassionate way, invites us to unload our guilt and shame, our burdens and sin, right at the foot of the cross daily, so that we may go forth upright and free to ask for anything we need from Him.

Oh friend, let's not put off this daily invitation a day longer. Let's strip down our excuses and simply show up before the throne of God … show up as we are before a God who loves us as we are.

## Cultivate

What is standing in the way of you approaching the throne of God with your honest heart, humble before Him?

# 9

I will fix my thoughts on whatever is true, and honorable, and right, and pure, and lovely, and admirable, and excellent, and praiseworthy.

*Finally, brothers and sisters, whatever is true, whatever is noble, whatever is right, whatever is pure, whatever is lovely, whatever is admirable—if anything is excellent or praiseworthy—think about such things.*
PHILIPPIANS 4:8

# *Connect*

Lord, how would our countenance change if we obeyed Your instructions to set our minds on whatever is true, right, pure, lovely, and admirable, and fix our thoughts on whatever is excellent and worthy of praise?

Would we be free of worry and anxiety?

Would we be free of jealousy and insecurity?

Would that make it easier to say adios to bitterness, anger, and resentment instead of ruminating over offenses?

If we really obeyed You in this area of minding our thoughts, what would happen to our emotional and spiritual health? Would joy fill our souls? Would peace reign in our hearts? God, what would happen to our physical bodies with less stress on our spirits?

---

**Lord, please forgive us for not obeying You, when all You're asking of us is to do what is best for our lives.**

---

Please give us a teachable heart and submitted spirit to do whatever You ask of us, even in our thought life.

In the strong name of Jesus, Amen.

# Consider

For a '90s girl like me, "whatever" comes out more like "www-whhhhhaaaatevvvvaaa," and always includes an eye roll. Regardless of our generational experience, the "whatever" we find in Philippians 4 offers a timeless application.

We can't go wrong to heed the wisdom of the Word to fill our mind with only that which is true, noble, right, pure, lovely, admirable, excellent, or praiseworthy.

If we were to get honest with one another, however, the "whatevers" filling our mind tend to not be quite in line with God's instructions. It's not just about the music we're listening to, books we're reading, or what we're watching on TV and viewing on the Internet. I definitely believe we need to consider those habits and make changes where appropriate. But we also need to be equally concerned about the conversations we engage in with others in real life and via a screen. Those "whatevers" matter just as much!

Is what we're listening to from those we live with, work with, and socialize with ... true, noble, right, pure, lovely, admirable, excellent, praiseworthy?

Is what we're reading on our social media feeds ... true, noble, right, pure, lovely, admirable, excellent, praiseworthy?

Wouldn't you agree that if the words being exchanged with those we're in relationships with, no matter how deep or superficial, don't echo the wisdom found in the Word, we've got a problem? So what does it look like to minimize those interactions or call each other out in a way that is loving, truthful, and grace-filled?

Are we surrounding ourselves with people and experiences that support our mission to think on ... whatever is true, noble, right, pure, lovely, admirable, excellent, praiseworthy?

Above all, we can't miss the most important part of the instruction from Philippians 4:8:

---

## We must be mindful of what we think about!

---

Oh yes, as we continue to move into a habit of taking captive our thoughts, we now have a sweet list of what to dwell upon … whatever is true, noble, right, pure, lovely, admirable, excellent, praiseworthy.

*Cultivate*

What can you do to begin the habit of dwelling on whatever is true, noble, right, pure, lovely, admirable, excellent, and praiseworthy?

# 10

I will choose to be kind and
speak kind words to others.

*Be kind and compassionate to one another,*
*forgiving each other, just as in Christ God forgave you.*
EPHESIANS 4:32

*Gracious words are a honeycomb,*
*sweet to the soul and healing to the bones.*
PROVERBS 16:24

# Connect

Heavenly Father, we come before You with a desire to be kind in our words and actions with everyone You put in our lives. But, Lord, it's hard!

We are all too easily rubbed the wrong way. We take offense, whether or not it is warranted, and react from a place of hurt. Kindness goes out the window when our wounds are pricked. Then our words become a weapon wielded without thought of consequence.

Forgive us, Lord! Change the way we speak and act toward others so that we become instruments of Your healing work. Make us quick to offer forgiveness, as You have done with us. Give us the courage to let an offense go and to trust You to reconcile accounts.

## Fill our mouths with gracious words, Oh Lord.

Make us vessels that pour sweetness onto others. Use us to heal wounds with kindness expressed in the words we speak, while making us quick to keep hurtful words from ever leaving our lips.

In the strong name of Jesus, Amen.

# Consider

This concept of being kind is actually something that has struck me afresh thanks to the perspective of a beautiful older woman who often spoke words of wisdom into our Bible study group. No matter the topic, Eileen would often provide the final contributing word, especially if another gal was really struggling with her faith.

"God is kind," she would say.

Again and again, Eileen spoke those three simple words as both a fact describing our loving, heavenly Father and as a promise for what to expect from Him in response to our troubles.

---

## God is kind.

---

Those three words have become not only a mantra playing over and over again in my heart and mind, but it has also become a mission with these two questions continually nagging at my spirit:

*How do my words exemplify the kindness of His words?*
*How do my actions convey His kindness to those I'm in relationship with?*

Is it time for these questions about how you're displaying the kindness of God to nag at your heart and mind too? My friend, we have such an amazing opportunity to be a testimony to the character and love of God by simply being kind in our words and actions.

# Cultivate

How can you go forth today, being kind as you seek to reflect the Father to those God has appointed you to be in relationship with?

BRAVE TOGETHER

# 11

I will be honest about my issues
with God and seek His help
(and counseling when needed)
for overcoming sin, strongholds,
and addictions.

*Don't think you are better than you really are. Be honest in your*
*evaluation of yourselves, measuring yourselves*
*by the faith God has given us.*

ROMANS 12:3

*Purify me from my sins, and I will be clean; wash me, and I will be*
*whiter than snow. Oh, give me back my joy again; you have broken*
*me—now let me rejoice. Don't keep looking at my sins.*
*Remove the stain of my guilt. Create in me a clean heart, O God.*
*Renew a loyal spirit within me.*

PSALM 51:7-10

# Connect

Heavenly Father, thank you that we can come to You with our issues … our sin, strongholds, and addictions. Thank you for the instruction and pattern You give us in Scripture for confessing our sins before You and walking in humble repentance.

Lord, we are grateful that David, a man after Your own heart who sinned gravely, inscribed words that echo the cry of our hearts. He declares who You are and what You're capable of while recognizing the way sin breaks our relationship with You. And He models confession and repentance for us, so that we may experience restoration with You.

Yes, Lord, You want honesty from our lips.

---

**God, may we humble ourselves
before You, seeking Your forgiveness
for the mess we make when we sin.**

---

Lord, cause us to keep short and honest accounts. Give us the courage to evaluate ourselves and to aggressively remove any obstacle from our lives that keeps us from living for You alone and reflecting Your glory to a watching world. May we be determined to live for You, unhindered by the sin that so easily entangles.

In the strong name of Jesus, Amen.

# *Consider*

I've discovered there's pretty much two different responses when it comes to matters of sin, strongholds, and addictions. Do you know what they are? Or which camp you fall in?

Some own it.

Some deny it.

Yep, it's that simple. Or it at least appears to be that simple on the surface. Think about it for a moment:

How does an alcoholic become sober?

What does a teen with anxiety do to find peace?

How does a woman with an eating disorder get healthy?

What can an angry mom do to become calmer?

The answer is the same for all. We first have to deal with the fact that we have an issue. We have to "own it" to heal from it. That's the first step, which is only possible when the root issue is tackled.

The root exists behind the fruit.

In the case of ongoing sin, strongholds, and addictions, the root is often a tangled web of pride encasing deeply infected emotional wounds and shame.

---

## Pride traps us in our sin, strongholds, and addictions.

---

It binds us up in darkness with lies. It keeps us from admitting we have a problem, running from the light, where the truth can set us free.

Pride causes us to deny that we need help. It's the worst place to dwell, and yet it's the place so many set up camp, remaining in destitution and desperation forever. I confess, it's beyond my understanding as to why. Since my early twenties, I've been bent on owning every bit of my sin and breaking free from every stronghold. I don't know if that is simply the mercy of God or the way His strong and fierce wiring in me works out for good. Regardless of the reason, I am so grateful to the Lord, because my willingness to seek Him honestly, and get counseling when necessary, has radically transformed my life and legacy. A day doesn't go by that I'm not aware of this twofold truth:

## God changes us from the inside out.

Through the study of Scripture, constant confession, years of prayer, and time in counseling, God has cleaned out my wounds and demolished the lies I've believed, causing the ticking bomb of anger within my heart to be deactivated. I'm no longer that angry mom. And, when it comes to strongholds, I'm also no longer that woman who feels she must produce in order to validate worth.

Bit by bit, as I own my stuff, God takes deep hold of my heart and transforms me into the woman He created me to become. Yes, it's an ongoing process. He's not done with me yet. And He's not done with you.

You are loved by God. You can step toward Him. He's inviting you to own your struggle, confess your sin, and break free from strongholds and addictions.

But He doesn't expect you to go at it alone. Seeking God for help, enlisting the support of family and friends, and getting professional help is more than okay. It's wise, my friend, and it will bear lasting fruit worth keeping.

### *Cultivate*

So which camp will you stick with? The camp of denial trapped by pride or the one wrapped in love, where owning your stuff leads to healing, growth, and the glory of God?

# 12

I will be the first to say I'm sorry, seek forgiveness, and offer forgiveness even when it's hard.

*But I confess my sins; I am deeply sorry for what I have done.*
PSALM 38:18

*Confess your sins to each other and pray for each other so that you may be healed. The earnest prayer of a righteous person has great power and produces wonderful results.*
JAMES 5:16

*Even if that person wrongs you seven times a day and each time turns again and asks forgiveness, you must forgive.*
Luke 17:4

## *Connect*

Lord God, we want to be quick to confess our sins to You. Please cultivate in us a heart that never hardens, so that we may always be deeply sorry for what we have done wrong in Your eyes. Lord, crush our pride so that we are willing to confess our sins to You and also those we can trust with our heart.

---

## God, thank you that honest confession leads to healing.

---

Thank you that the earnest prayer of a righteous person has great power and produces wonderful results. Yes, Lord, we hope to see those results in our own lives!

Lord, it's not easy to walk in forgiveness with those who have sinned against us. But You request that offering forgiveness, even seven times a day, to the ones who have offended us is a must. Oh Lord, really? It's so hard. Please enable us to be people who forgive quickly and often.

In the strong name of Jesus, Amen.

# Consider

My youngest daughter had just finished helping my middle daughter study for her chemistry test by quizzing her on her flash cards. When all was said and done, she confessed, "Chemistry is so hard. I don't think it will make sense to me even when I'm in your class, Daddy." Yes, my kiddos have the blessing of living with their chemistry teacher. My husband's response to my daughter took me by surprise.

"It's only hard because you can't see it."

She pressed him, "What do you mean I can't see it?"

He answered, "Well, you can't see the why ... the process of getting to the answer is abstract."

How true, not only about chemistry but also about forgiveness. In the case of forgiveness, we may never see the outcome clearly. All the preceding steps may also be obscure; however, the fruit is always visible. There's a hurt inflicted, a careless grazing of pain against the heart, or maybe an outright sin. Regardless of the offense, a wound is caused and it takes on a power all it's own, as it becomes infected and attempts to destroy the life of its victim.

---

## Unforgiveness leaves the most obvious, regrettable marks on a person's life.

---

Have you noticed the way unforgiveness manifests itself in bitterness and resentment, anger and a critical spirit? Have you seen the way unforgiveness causes isolation and despair, depression and anxiety? Or the way it becomes the source of feeling defeated and defensive?

Unforgiveness makes a mess of our lives, whether it's the guilt we carry over our own offenses or the wound caused by another that we fail to have Him treat.

Like a chemist, we need to be aware of elements involved. Yes, we need to own our stuff ... our hurt as well as our sin, as we talked about in principle #11. The first step always has to be in naming the pain before God, and then seeking His truth for dealing with our hurt. The second step is simple obedience. God says to seek forgiveness from Him when we've sinned. Could it be any plainer? And the third step is choosing to forgive those who have sinned against us, regardless of their willingness to receive it.

---

**When we forgive the ones who hurt us, we're setting them free for God to respond with justice and mercy.**

---

Could our own response be better than that? NO! And I speak as one with experience. Oh yes, I know this dance of forgiveness well, as I've walked this road, my friend.

Forgiveness is the secret to living a life of freedom.

In moving through the process of forgiveness with the Lord, we can live free from guilt and shame, released from pain and hurt.

Forgiveness is like a feather floating toward the ground, gracefully landing wherever the wind carries it. It's unhindered. Burdenedless. And simply free.

## Cultivate

Is it time for you to be set free today, simply by obeying God in this journey of forgiveness?

# 13

I will remember that I am fearfully
and wonderfully made, not on accident,
but on purpose for a good purpose.

*For you created my inmost being; you knit me together
in my mother's womb. I praise you because I am fearfully and wonderfully made; your works are wonderful, I know that full well My
frame was not hidden from you when I was made in the secret
place, when I was woven together in the depths of the earth. Your
eyes saw my unformed body; all the days ordained for me
were written in your book before one of them came to be.*
PSALM 139:13-17

*For we are God's handiwork, created in Christ Jesus to
do good works, which God prepared in advance for us to do.*
EPHESIANS 2:10

# Connect

Heavenly Father, shall we even bother speaking our own words when the psalmist has so clearly captured what should be the song of our hearts.

Yes, Lord, You formed us.

Yes, Lord, You made us fearfully and marvelously.

Yes, Lord You conceived us long before we took our first breath and emerged into this world. Thank you, Lord, that You know every hair on our heads, every inch of our bodies.

Thank you, God, for knowing each one of us like no one else does and loving us all the same.

---

**Thank you for beginning a good work in us and promising to carry it out to completion.**

---

Yes, Lord, we agree with Your Word that You have a purpose for our lives. Please, God, write Your story as You desire.

In the strong name of Jesus, Amen.

# *Consider*

Will you take a minute to slow down your mind and calm your heart in order to soak up today's scriptures? It's so easy to skim ahead … and miss the Holy Spirit's prompting to go deeper. If you've been walking with the Lord as a Bible-reading gal for some time, it's even more of a temptation to rush through the familiar passages. Wouldn't you agree?

I suspect that for most of us, Psalm 139 is just that … too familiar. Too often quoted. But also too often overlooked. I know I'm quick to quote the highlights …

*He knows me.*
*I'm fearfully and wonderfully made.*
*He searches the heart.*
*He knows all the hairs on my head.*

But, there is so much more in this passage, my friend. Isn't that the beauty of Scripture? Through the power of the Holy Spirit, God can bring alive His truth in fresh ways every time we read. So what is God speaking to your heart today from Psalm 139 and Ephesians 2:10?

As I read it slowly and purposefully, I was struck by this one portion of verse 16:

*… all the days ordained for me were written in your book before one of them came to be.*

I suspect the fact that I'm currently working on a devotional book for Harvest House makes this notion quite personal. Each day when I sit down to write, I have to spend much time in prayer and waiting on God to show me a verse to focus on and a story worth telling. I have no idea as to what will be written in this little book God has tasked me with the privilege of writing. I can't even conceive of what it would be like to know all the stories in advance! And yet God does.

---

## God knows our stories and the ones we've yet to uncover.

---

God even knew that as I was crafting this devotional, I'd cross paths with a precious woman enrolled in my life coaching training course, who found out about it through reading *Meet the New You*. She believed I was an answer to her prayers, sharing that my book gave her a fresh sense of purpose after coming through a season of deep loss. And I believed she was very much an answer to my prayers, because it's my deepest desire that God would use my words to encourage even one woman in the journey of finding renewed purpose in her life.

God can write our stories simultaneously because He is able to do exceedingly and abundantly more than we can ask or imagine (Ephesians 3:20)!

What God does with our lives is for His great purposes. Yet we spend so much time wondering about our purpose because we can't see the end. What if we lived with the end in mind?

What if we lived in such a way that we found our hope and purpose in knowing that God is always busy writing our story while we're busy living it?

## Cultivate

How can you embrace a perspective shift to see the value God has sown into your life while trusting that He who began a good work in you will bring it to completion?

# 14

I will commit to accountability relationships with one to two other women.

*Run from anything that stimulates youthful lusts.*
*Instead, pursue righteous living, faithfulness, love,*
*and peace. Enjoy the companionship of those who*
*call on the Lord with pure hearts.*
2 Timothy 2:22

# Connect

Lord God, thank you that You've created us for friendship. Thank you that Your design is for us to not go through life alone. You long for us to have companionship with those who call upon You with a pure heart.

---

## God, we ask for You to provide us with authentic and meaningful friendships.

---

God, give us the courage to reach out beyond our own insecurities.

Help us get creative in the ways we go about finding friends and cultivating lasting relationships.

God, in our pursuit of friendships, we pray that You will give us wisdom and discernment. Help us to flee from those who might cause us to stumble. Bring us into relationship with those who will hold us accountable in the mission of right living, faithfulness, love, and peace.

In the strong name of Jesus, Amen.

# Consider

It was a question I didn't see coming.

*Well, who are your friends?*

*Who do you spend time with?*

I could feel the warm flush of embarrassment take over my face. How could I answer this question authentically and still save face? I couldn't really, so I fumbled out a few garbled words in a feeble attempt to explain my situation. The reality is that I don't really have a group of friends, yet. It's more like pockets of friendships that are still forming not even two years after moving to this new place. There are definitely precious women God has brought into my life, and I see the potential of deep and lasting friendships … but making friends takes time.

So what do we do with this call from God to enjoy the companionship of those who call on the Lord with a pure heart?

Well, I think we start by first admitting that it's a good call meant for our benefit. It also is a call that requires a dedicated effort on our part. For the majority of us, godly friendships don't just come knocking on our door. We have to make ourselves available to cultivate friendships and be willing to risk a rejection by pursuing time together again and again.

---

**Pure in heart companions come in many forms and they are all equally valuable.**

---

So for some of us, we'll find the connection points by going to Bible study, even if "the study" isn't something we'd choose to do on our own. It may look like setting aside a time each week for connection, not always with a new face but giving up casting the net wide to focus on a few. That's really the secret to cultivating accountability friendships that are more than surface deep.

Your connecting points have to be more than once a month to really get to know each other.

I have to confess that one of the reasons I haven't felt the need to cultivate many "in real life" friendships is because of the way I'm so tightly connected to women around the country. Do you feel this way too? Using Voxer, along with texting and social media, enables me to stay tied to the hearts of dear sisters, even if we never get to walk in the park side-by-side together.

These kinds of friendships are incredibly valuable for accountability, prayer, and encouragement, but there's nothing like sharing a meal together with friends who live only a town away.

Both are part of God's plans for us to find the kinds of women we can build soul-filling, life-changing accountability relationships with.

## Cultivate

How can you embrace both real life and online connections in a way that builds a community of godly companionship in your life?

# 15

I will make it a habit to speak in psalms, hymns, and spiritual songs.

*Let the message about Christ, in all its richness, fill your lives. Teach and counsel each other with all the wisdom he gives. Sing psalms and hymns and spiritual songs to God with thankful hearts.*

COLOSSIANS 3:16

# Connect

Lord God, please allow Your message to dwell richly in our lives and to fill us completely.

God, may Your truth permeate our hearts and minds to such a degree that more of Your spirit overflows from us organically and powerfully.

---

**Lord, we want Your Word to be alive in us so that we may teach and counsel with your wisdom and not our own thoughts or opinions.**

---

God, how dramatically different our lives would be if we spoke in psalms, hymns, and spiritual songs … singing to You continually with a thankful heart.

Lord, tune our ears to Your Word and open our hearts to receive the fullness of Christ so that our voices may come together as one as we sing songs of thankfulness to You for Your love and wisdom that You freely give to all who ask.

In the strong name of Jesus, Amen.

# *Consider*

I'm sure we looked like any other pair of friends catching up over a cup of coffee, but what you might not have noticed from afar is what binds us together. It was more than just history.

We met only a few days after our youngest babes where born. She was determined to make a place for herself in my friendship circle at a time when I really wasn't interested in growing it larger. I already felt pulled in too many directions. But by the grace of God, she was persistent, especially in her desires to get me to work with her to start a moms' group.

I'm not sure how she broke through my "no, thank you, not now, not ever," but she did.

For two years, we met biweekly at her home with doors swung wide open to any woman who wanted to spend time digging into Scripture. We called it WOWAM … Women With a Mission … and I had a big vision for it to be the next women's ministry taking over the United States, while she just wanted us to focus on the gals in our local community.

We both agreed, however, that our mission was about growing deeper in our personal relationship with the Lord while encouraging one another to walk out our faith with our families and friends.

Our little group was really an attempt at sharing what we already found worth treasuring in our friendship.

*A friendship in which we were passionate about encouraging one another in our faith.*

*A friendship that invited the message of Christ to grow in our hearts.*

*A friendship in which we sometimes became each others teacher and other times coach, striving always to speak out the wisdom of God.*

*A friendship where our words often sounded like the psalmist, echoing truths of the greatest hymns and songs we'd belt out each Sunday at church.*

More than a decade later … and now living in separate states … our friendship is still one that I count on to set my heart right before the Lord and call me deeper into a relationship with Him. That's because it's upon the fullness of Christ dwelling richly in us that we are bound together.

Whether across the miles by phone or across the table from each other sharing a cup of coffee, she is my sister in Christ who always speaks to me in psalms, hymns, and spiritual songs with the wisdom of God guiding her words … because the fullness of Christ most definitely dwells in her heart.

## *Cultivate*

How is God calling you to cultivate and invest in friendships that fulfill the call of Colossians 3:16?

# 16

I will strive to do everything
for the glory of God.

*Whatever you do—whether you eat or
drink or not—do it all to the glory of God!*
1 Corinthians 10:31 THE VOICE

# Connect

Lord God, we want to live in such a way that whether we eat or drink ... or not ... that we do it all for Your glory.

Whether we go to work or stay home, that we do it all for Your glory.

Whether we serve at church or volunteer in an organization, that we do it all for Your glory.

Whether we engage in one-on-one conversations or speak before a crowd, that we do it all for Your glory.

Whether we love on a friend or reach out to a stranger, that we do it all for Your glory.

Whether we clean our home or wash the dishes or fold the laundry, that we do it all for Your glory.

Whether we change a dirty diaper or drive an aging parent to a doctor's appointment, that we do it all for Your glory.

---

**Whatever You have for us to do, on any day and at any time, we pray that our motive will always be to do it for Your glory.**

---

In the strong name of Jesus, Amen.

# *Consider*

What does it mean to you to do something for the glory of God? I ask because I think it's so important to slow ourselves down and think long and hard about the expressions we use so often, because maybe they've lost their meaning.

So may I encourage you to take a moment, and sit quietly with the Lord. Close your eyes. Take a deep breath. And think about this question:

---

## What do you mean when you say you want to live for the glory of God?

---

If this is your mission, how are you going about fulfilling it?

When I close my eyes and reflect on living for God's glory, I actually think of that locker room scene from *Facing the Giants*, when Coach Grant Taylor challenges the boys to play football and live their lives in such a way that they give God their best so that He always gets the glory.

Coach Taylor asked the boys a question: "What is the purpose of this team?" What if you took that question and applied it to your life?

1. What's your main purpose?
2. Is your life all about you?
3. Is it about how you can look good?
4. Is it about you getting glory or God?

Coach Taylor explained to his team that they had an opportunity to play in such a way as to give God their best all the time, on and off the field. Their effort counted for something, but it was their focus on doing it for the glory of God that mattered most.

Isn't the same true for us? Are we utterly devoted to God in every way, in every relationship, in every task? Are we willing to give everything our best, but with the motive that God gets all the glory?

Friend, if we belong to Christ, then shouldn't everything we do be out of a desire to please God and reveal to the world the One they need most?

## Cultivate

What is one attitude adjustment or habit change you can take to move your heart into a place of doing everything for the glory of God?

# 17

I will be a woman of my word.

*All you need to say is simply 'Yes' or 'No';*
*anything beyond this comes from the evil one.*
MATTHEW 5:37

# *Connect*

God, as emotional beings, we're driven all too often by what we feel. And our feelings all too often sway our decisions. Our "yes" becomes a "well, now I can't" and our "no" becomes, "well, maybe I can."

Oh Lord, we need Your help.

There is no way our decisions can be steadfast without You, especially when the enemy is out to make us hypocrites and cause division in our relationships over broken promises.

Please give us the wisdom to wait until we're sure before we say "yes." And give us the strength to say "no," even if the pull or pressure is strong to give in.

---

## God, please make us women of our word ... women yielded to Your Word.

---

In the strong name of Jesus, Amen.

# Consider

I hate going back on my word, and yet, I've been in that kind of situation more times than I care to count. One particular experience stands out most with both regret and yet gratefulness to the Lord. I made a commitment to serve a three-year term on the women's ministry team at my church. How I coveted that opportunity for more than a decade, which should've been clue number one that my motives might have skewed my ability to make a wise choice.

Oh, I prayed and sought counsel before making the decision, but the problem was that I was easily swayed by the desire for validation and value, for acceptance and approval. Even though I was aware that the responsibilities would impact my priorities as a momma of littles, I was also itching for something to put my hands to besides housework and mothering. Looking back, I wonder if I only sought advice from those I thought would support my decision to say "yes."

Oh yes, even in seeking counsel, we can be manipulative. Have you been guilty of doing the same?

One older gal said to me, "It'll be good for you to get out and do something for yourself." Another woman said, "Your children need to know you have a life apart from them." Another said, "You'll be able to give more back to your family if you're doing something to stimulate your mind." And the one response that was most compelling to me was, "You'll be teaching your girls by example what it looks like to serve."

In seeking counsel, I received plenty of advice. But I didn't need advice. I needed wisdom. I needed discernment. I needed to be challenged to consider my limitations, my family's needs, and our core values.

None of these well-meaning gals took into consideration the intricacies of my life or what God wanted of me. They imparted their values, and that, my friend, is never helpful. That's also the problem with advice-giving! And it's why I'm so passionate about the value of life coaching, which builds upon the principles of asking and answering open-ended questions to arrive at the ah-ha solution.

Questions like these would have made the world of difference:

- What will it cost you to say "no"?
- What will it cost you to say "yes"?
- What about this role makes you want to say "yes"?
- What will be the impact on your family?
- How do you feel about the timing of this opportunity?
- How do you feel you can contribute based on the state of your heart? Spiritual maturity? Emotional reserves? Physical and practical limitations?
- Is there another way you can satisfy your desire to get involved without making such a commitment?
- What does your husband have to say about this?
- How does this fit with your core values?
- How does this fit with your family's mission and priorities?

If I had taken the time to consider even a few of these questions, I would have said "no" because the answer was as plain as day. It was not a good fit for my kiddos in that season of their life. Plus, the way I was currently serving with my husband and our mission as a family to be "all in" with him through serving at a boarding school was already consuming. Ultimately, I had to find that out for myself in a very painful, teary, year-long heartache that began within months of saying "yes."

My pride and commitment to be a woman of my word, kept me hanging on for another six months, even though I knew it was damaging my relationship with my middle daughter. She needed me in a way I didn't want to be needed. And it took a mighty act of the Lord to convict me to the point of being willing to let go of the ministry role, along with the grace and urging from my husband that it was okay to resign.

It was the most embarrassing and humbling time of my life. I felt like I failed my church and the women on my team. I felt like I failed God. It took years for the shame to be replaced by grace, as I realized that God was teaching me a valuable lesson that has proved beneficial a bazillion times over.

While I had to turn my "yes" into a "no," I came to see how important it is for my "yes" and "no" to be more thoughtfully prayed through and guarded against the enemy's attempt to derail my life and God's purposes.

---

**Yes, our flesh won't always heed the Spirit's leading, and our motives can easily derail us from the course God wants us to take.**

---

Our friends can lead us in the wrong direction. But the good news is that God can take our yielded hearts and accomplish His redemptive purposes in our lives as we seek to be women of our word.

## *Cultivate*

When it comes to making decisions, how have you been derailed by the enemy? What can you do in the future to make wiser choices, so that your "yes" and "no" can be your word?

# 18

I will seek God for a changed heart before trying to change my circumstances.

*I will give you a new heart and put a new spirit in you; I will remove from you your heart of stone and give you a heart of flesh.*
EZEKIEL 36:26

# Connect

Lord God, Your kindness is beyond words. How do we thank you for being willing to take our hearts of stone and turn them into hearts of flesh? What a miracle of all miracles!

---

## God, when You change a heart, You change a life and a legacy.

---

And when You, Lord, change a legacy, You change a generation.

God, we yield our hearts to You. Do Your work in us and through us! Change what You must change in us, from the inside out.

In the strong name of Jesus, Amen.

# Consider

We were nearing the end of a casual dinner on our patio, where the conversation went deep with our kids over the life we once led. Oh, how we missed boarding school community and rhythms, as much as we were all learning to embrace the joys of this new life we were living. The girls and my son told story after story about recounting how their lives were shaped by their experiences in that community. I also could see how it impacted our parenting approach through teaching me about the character of God and the biblical values I wanted to see shape my children's lives.

## Are there people God has used in your life experience to shape you … and your heart?

The greatest impact of that community was how the Lord used so many people to transform me from the inside out! He turned my stony heart to flesh (Ezekiel 36:26). Maybe you know this part of my story and are wondering why I'm telling it again. Because, my friend, it is still part of my story unfolding today. The journey and the fruit. The yielding and the waiting.

My heart was so full of junk, so hardened by wounds, but I had no idea. Now I am fully aware of what a hardened heart feels like. I can tell you there are still parts to be unloaded.

Once I thought, *This is just who I am and who I'll always be.* Is that how you feel?

Hard. Angry. Hurtful. Bitter. Unforgiving. Ashamed. Guilty.

That might have been who I once was, but the good news is that's not who I am today. And that's not who you have to be either. I have my moments of ugliness and flesh-ruling behavior, but it is no longer the norm.

The Lord entered deep into my hardened heart through truth-with-love words spoken by friends and mentors and most critically, my husband, at a time in which I was ready to hear what they had to say. They had already proven their love to me, which laid a foundation for them to speak truth to my soul. With the help of counseling, I began to unpack my stony heart, laying one offense after another before the Lord. He transformed the lies into truth and showed me how to continue that pattern as I began embracing biblically rooted attitudes and habits that lead to the kind of real life change I describe in *Meet the New You* … change that is also possible for you!

Yes, God turned my heart of stone to a heart full of His love, grace, kindness, and truth. In doing so, He changed my legacy. Over time. Over years. Day by day. Moment by moment. And it is a testimony of His work in me … a work He also wants to do in you.

It really is His miracle.

I pray you'll be brave and say yes to the Lord's transformative work in your heart, day by day, moment by moment. Because when we begin with yes to the Lord, we say yes to impacting the next generation for His glory.

## Cultivate

How is the Lord inviting you to yield your heart to Him, so that He can turn it from stone to flesh?

# 19

I will guard my heart by considering
what I expose myself to each day.

*Above all else, guard your heart,*
*for everything you do flows from it.*
Proverbs 4:23

# Connect

Lord, we pray that You will show us what it means to guard our hearts since everything we do flows from it.

Enable us to recognize the potential for heart damage that can happen when we expose ourselves to situations and circumstances that are damaging to our soul.

God, help us see the influence of what "plays" on repeat on our screens and in our ears.

---

**Lord, give us a sensitivity to the Holy Spirit's leading and a quickness to heed any conviction You provide for our protection.**

---

In the strong name of Jesus, Amen.

# Consider

Guard your heart.

Because everything flows from it.

Could it be any simpler of an instruction from the Lord? We've got to watch what goes in, because that's what will come out. We bump into this principle not only in the Old Testament but also in the New Testament:

> *For the mouth speaks what the heart is full of.*
> MATTHEW 12:34B

> *A good man brings good things out of the good stored up in his heart, and an evil man brings evil things out of the evil stored up in his heart. For the mouth speaks what the heart is full of.*
> LUKE 6:45

So what are we storing up in our hearts? Is it pain and hurt? Is it unforgiveness that desperately needs His healing work?

What are we exposing ourselves to every day? Especially on our screens. Oh yes, it affects the heart.

What are we watching and listening to on repeat? What are the undertones and overtones coming through … in music and podcasts, TV and Netflix, movies and YouTube?

What are we hearing from those we're in relationship with? Those we work with? Is it affirming the Word of God or a group-think culture steeped in criticism, negativity, and the ways of this world? Oh, I know these questions can make us squirm, as they trigger a sense of legalism and fear of isolation.

Wouldn't you agree that the minute we start judging what is right for ourselves, we find ourselves tempted to make policies, rules, and procedures for everyone else?

At the heart of it, we don't want to miss out on something everyone else seems to be enjoying … or at least participating in. We don't want to be noticed for being different. We don't want to be judged or criticized, questioned or ostracized. Right?

But when we refuse to evaluate what's going into our hearts, we're also refusing to recognize the impact of what is coming out of us. And what's coming out of us is what shapes our testimony, our influence, our legacy.

---

**If our ultimate goal is to glorify God, then being intentional about what we allow to fill our hearts really becomes about submitting to how God wants to use us in this world.**

---

Isn't that an interesting thought? A simple instruction about guarding our hearts, which appears to be just about us, isn't about us at all.

## Cultivate

When you think about this instruction to guard your heart, because of the impact of what will flow from it, what comes to mind? What is one thing you ought to shield your heart from?

# 20

I will pursue a life of whole-heart, whole-mind, whole-body purity.

*Teach me your ways, O Lord,*
*that I may live according to your truth!*
*Grant me purity of heart, so that I may honor you.*
PSALM 86:11

*Give honor to marriage, and remain*
*faithful to one another in marriage.*
*God will surely judge people who are*
*immoral and those who commit adultery.*
HEBREWS 13:4

# Connect

Father God, thank you for teaching us Your ways and showing us how to live according to Your truth. Thank you for granting us purity of heart, so that we may honor You.

---

## God, work in our hearts to give us a desire to honor You in every way.

---

Lord, please give us purity of heart and a commitment to honor You, whether we are single or married.

Give us insight and wisdom and determination so that we can be faithful in our marriages.

God, protect us from distraction and temptation that will be detrimental to our pursuit of whole-life purity.

In the strong name of Jesus, Amen.

# *Consider*

Would you agree that "purity" is a buzz word in Christian circles? It is almost like a dirty word when it really should be a principle that graces our thoughts and infuses every part of our lives.

Would you also agree that there's a kind of purity bandwagon, where the policy is "don't talk, don't tell, don't do"? Is that how you were raised? Is that the pattern of communication you feel like you're stuck in today?

Or do you feel hit with condemnation, since your journey was anything but pure? I got over that kind of burden a long, long time ago—but I still remember it well.

Do you feel nervous about how to instill purity in your tween and teenage sons and daughters, wondering if it is hypocritical to say, "Don't do this, even though I did"? Or maybe you fear that talking about purity, and defining what is not, will plant ideas and lead to a kind of purity rebellion?

Friend, I've come to learn after all these years in mentoring tweens and teens, and moving through my own journey of healing, that talking about purity doesn't make one more pure or less pure.

## The pursuit of purity is something each of us needs to reconcile before God for ourselves.

Purity, at its core, is really about honoring the Lord with our mind, body, and soul. It's not about a set of rules. It's not about being better than "that person over there," even though that's the mockery purity has become in our culture. Did you know there's even a test to assess your purity? Oh yes, college students use the Rice Purity Test for bragging rights. I warn you, don't look at it. You'll end up sick and heartbroken. The test gives a numerical score based on how you answer the questions. Those who want to tout their purity boast about a high score, while those who feel it's cooler to be on the rebellious side of things brag about their low score. But when did purity become about a number?

Purity is about so much more than simply keeping your pants on until you're married. I know, crass, but true. We have pigeonholed purity into mantras that neglect to see the essence of whole life purity.

Pursuing purity isn't just about not having sex outside of marriage.

It's about the way we are interacting with others, whether we are single or married.

Purity is the pursuit of holiness as a child of God.

And purity is as much about what you take in through your eyes and ears as what you do with your body. It's about what you expose your heart and mind and soul to each and every day.

If purity is about honoring God, then that's not something we need to make up rules about. He's already given us everything we need to know about how to honor Him through His Word. There's no need to come up with a new set of terms. Rather, it's about digging deeper into our relationship with God through faith in Jesus, inviting the Holy Spirit to lead us into whole-life, whole-mind, whole-body purity.

## Cultivate

What is God speaking to your heart about your own purity? How about tackling the topic with the tweens and teens in your life?

# 21

I will carefully consider the
words I choose to speak.

*The words you say will either acquit you or condemn you.*

MATTHEW 12:37

*But the words you speak come from the
heart—that's what defiles you.*
MATTHEW 15:18

# Connect

Father God, our words matter so much to You, and yet how carelessly we use them. Please forgive us for not paying attention to the implications of what we say. Prompt us to take notice of our words and seriously consider where they come from.

God, we know our words are not the root of the problem, but it's what is going on in our hearts and minds that causes us to speak as we do. It's the words we speak, from the heart, that defile us.

---

## Oh Lord, please make our hearts pure.

---

Please cause us to carefully guard what goes in, so that what comes out of our mouths gives You all honor and glory.

In the strong name of Jesus, Amen.

# Consider

My father always said, "Loose lips sink ships." While I didn't know where that saying came from, the message got across. We need to be careful about the words coming out of our mouths because we can all too easily say things we regret. Can you relate?

---

## Our words matter much.

---

Yes, much, much, much more than we care to acknowledge.

As a culture, we've become even careless and crass, disregarding the setting and circumstances in which we tout our opinions.

Could it be that we've totally lost our filter thanks to reality TV and talk show banter?

How many hours have we spent listening to the running commentary of a prospective house buyer critiquing a space? How about the many opinions we ingest about a particular chef's cooking? Or about a singer's singing? A politician's politics?

The kinds of non-consequential running of the mouth we witness on TV reaps a grave reward if it manifests in our personal relationships.

I believe we've bought into the lie that we're entitled to share our opinions with as much criticism, sarcasm, and enthusiasm as we like, without regard for whether our words are of any benefit. Our words matter much to the one they are being spoken to. Our commentary and critiques leave identity-stinging wounds.

The truth is sticks and stones will break our bones AND words WILL harm us. Don't you agree? Even though the wounds from words are hard to see, they can linger for a lifetime. Those hidden word-wounds, when left untreated, become wounding words. Yes, the wounded wound.

Is that why it's so important to take stock of our words and what is going on in our hearts? Our words will either acquit us or condemn us before the Lord. I don't know about you, but I don't want to be condemned.

Yes, getting our hearts right before the Lord is a daily discipline. It's not only about reconciling what was, but it's about confessing what is. Every old wound and every little offense needs to be handed over to the Lord so that our hearts can be purified by God's extravagant love and amazing grace. Only then, my friend, will we be able to speak the kind of words that will acquit us.

## Cultivate

How have you been loose with your lips in a way that has caused harm? Is it a matter of carelessness? Is it time to consider the overflow of what is in your heart?

# 22

I will watch my words to
consider the state of my heart.

*The right-living think before they speak,*
*but wrongdoers simply spew evil.*
PROVERBS 15:28 THE VOICE

*It's the same with people. A person full of goodness in his heart*
*produces good things; a person with an evil reservoir in his*
*heart pours out evil things. The heart overflows in the words*
*a person speaks; your words reveal what's within your heart.*
LUKE 6:45 THE VOICE

# Connect

Father God, this heart-words thing is pretty important to You. It seems that so many scriptures remind us to be careful about what we speak, and that the words that slip out of our mouths actually reveal the state of our heart.

So often it isn't until those words come out that we actually recognize there's something in our heart that needs Your attention.

And then, it feels too late. The damage is done.

---

**Please, God, give us the courage to own our words, no matter when they come out.**

---

May we seek You quickly for healing and hope so that there can be better overflow from our hearts. Father, please give us humility to seek forgiveness from those we might have hurt with our carelessly spoken words, too.

In the strong name of Jesus, Amen.

# Consider

I confess, it really does feel like we're going around the same mountain again and again as we tackle this topic about minding our words and the state of our hearts.

---

## It must be that the Lord really wants us to understand the power of our words and the matters of the heart.

---

Wouldn't it be nice if we could tackle it once and for all? And yet, the truth is that our hearts are in a constant state of flux. The triggers are endless. From something someone says to the way we catch a glimpse of ourselves in a mirror. To the color of the sky or even smell of summer in the air. People trigger us. Seasons trigger us. Moments trigger us. But I find one of the worst triggers to be social media. Is this the case for you too?

I came to the conclusion that Facebook is a drain on my soul long before the reports came out testifying about its impact. The research I did on social media and screens was enough to confirm the problem, which spurred me on to more intentionally manage how I use it. It's not that it is just a jealousy trigger for me, as I see the beautiful vacations and home remodels and social gatherings my "friends" are all blessed with experiencing. It's also that I'm keenly aware that my own postings may trigger others the exact same way, which often makes me not want to post at all. I don't want to cause a sister to stumble. Not in real life and not through a screen.

You and I both know full well that what we see on the screen is one-dimensional, and yet, it doesn't seem to be a truth that stops our heart-ugly response. No one posts about their failing marriages and wayward children and their struggle with chronic pain, depression, anxiety, or inability to ever lose the weight.

We only share our successes, while hiding our everyday losses.

I battle the jealousy trigger with gratitude, along with minimizing my usage, but it's actually the posting for prayers around health crisis situations that wrecks my heart even more. I feel hard and deep for those battling for their lives. I want to offer words of encouragement and prayer support. However, I don't think God ever intended my heart to carry the weight of 1,000 "friends" on my shoulders. Statistically speaking, the more people I know, the more I'll be acquainted with pain. Have you felt this too?

My heart isn't able to endure news of another diagnosis every day of the week. It's this kind of news that makes me anxious and irritable, moody and short-tempered. Can you relate? I get off my screen with a heavy heart and then hurt the ones in my midst with biting remark.

The fact is that there are so many triggers that cause our heart to go awry and our words to be regrettable. Since our hearts soak everything up, shall we be proactive in minimizing the everyday triggers, especially the ones that come from social media exposure?

## Cultivate

What are the triggers that set off your heart and cause your words to flow from a place of pain rather than His love?

# 23

I will do all that I can to live
in peace with others.

*Do all that you can to live in peace with everyone.*

Romans 12:18

# Connect

Father God, Your Word is so plain in instructing us that we should do all we can to live in peace with everyone. But what exactly does that look like?

Please open our ears to hear Your voice, so that we may heed You when You prompt us to pursue peace in our relationships.

Keep us from stewing in our own pride and selfishness.

Keep us from recounting offenses.

Keep us from rehearsing rebuttals.

---

**Move our hearts toward peace by filling our hearts with more of You, so that we may live in peace with everyone.**

---

In the strong name of Jesus, Amen.

# *Consider*

Have you ever focused on one point of scripture and felt totally at a lost understanding the meaning and application? Take this verse, for example.

---

## **Live. In. Peace. With. Others.**

---

Oh help us, sweet Jesus!

If you're the type who rolls easily along, this command from God is not such a big deal. But for someone like me, who rolls like a square log … *thump, thump, thump* … it feels impossible. That's not to say I don't crave peace. I do want peace to permeate all my relationships. Yet more often than not, I find myself in the middle of a conflict. For the life of me, I can't figure out why. Can you relate?

Maybe it's a personality thing, in that I don't mind speaking my mind. Maybe it's a spiritual gifting, in that my sense of discernment causes me to bring attention to matters someone else may not notice. Or maybe, I find myself in conflict because I'm not heeding the other portions of scripture leading up to and following this particular verse from Romans 12. Take a look at it in context:

> *Don't just pretend to love others. Really love them. Hate what is wrong. Hold tightly to what is good. Love each other with genuine affection, and take delight in honoring each other. Never be lazy, but work hard and serve the Lord enthusiastically. Rejoice in our confident hope. Be patient in trouble, and keep on praying. When God's people are in need, be ready to help them. Always be eager to practice hospitality.*
>
> ROMANS 12:9-13

Do you see all the "how to" instructions for what it takes to live in peace? Even though we are to hate what is wrong and hold tightly to what is good, we also have to love each other with genuine affection and honor one another. Ahem, no sarcasm. No biting words. We have to be patient and prayerful, willing to help in times of need and practice hospitality with everyone. By doing so, we set the stage for peace.

This next verse packs an even more powerful punch:

> *Bless those who persecute you. Don't curse them;*
> *pray that God will bless them.*
> ROMANS 12:14

How about this modern translation: Bless those who make us miserable. Oh yes! And go the distance to not curse them but pray for them. It's a totally counter cultural approach and opposite from the nature of our flesh. Instead of fighting back, we are called to blessing and prayer. How? By the grace of God, we can press on to embrace these instructions:

> *Be happy with those who are happy, and weep with those who*
> *weep. Live in harmony with each other. Don't be too proud to enjoy*
> *the company of ordinary people. And don't think you know it all!*
> *Never pay back evil with more evil. Do things in such a way that*
> *everyone can see you are honorable. Do all that you can to live in*
> *peace with everyone.*
> ROMANS 12:15-18

It's not too hard to be happy with the happy and weep with those weeping. But, oh my, how we all can be so arrogant or uppity about who we should spend time with. Our tendency is not toward kindness and honor, but revenge, as these next verses describe.

*Dear friends, never take revenge. Leave that to the righteous anger of God. For the Scriptures say, "I will take revenge; I will pay them back," says the Lord. Instead, "If your enemies are hungry, feed them. If they are thirsty, give them something to drink. In doing this, you will heap burning coals of shame on their heads." Don't let evil conquer you, but conquer evil by doing good.*

ROMANS 12:19-21

Yes, God gives us so many practical ways to strive toward living in peace with those we do life with every day and with those who are just awful to us.

But true peace is only possible if we heed the call by submitting to the Spirit's leading and allow the fullness of Jesus to manifest Himself in our lives.

In our flesh, we'll fail. But through the power of Christ at work in our hearts and minds, we can embrace this call. Since He is the Prince of Peace, why not give Him full access to do His work in our lives rather than struggling to manifest a peace in ourselves that will never compare?

## Cultivate

As you consider the different ways God instructs us to strive after peace, which point do you feel He is calling you to focus on this week?

# 24

I will remember that my life is a story God is writing for others to see Him.

*Clearly, you are a letter from Christ showing the result of our ministry among you. This "letter" is written not with pen and ink, but with the Spirit of the living God. It is carved not on tablets of stone, but on human hearts.*

2 CORINTHIANS 3:3

# Connect

Father God, thank you for the way You write Your story on our hearts.

Thank you for not using pen and ink, which can be destroyed and thrown away, but choosing to write with Your Spirit. It's like a permanent sharpie marker, recording evidence of Your faithfulness, provision, forgiveness, grace, truth, and redemption through the story You're writing in our lives.

---

**God, we give You our hearts,
once again on this journey, and we ask
You to write Your story for Your glory.**

---

In the strong name of Jesus, Amen.

# Consider

If you've been a follower of More to Be since the beginning, you might remember one of my first resources, *StoryHearts: Embracing the Handwriting of God*. It was a downloadable devotional inviting you to consider the story God might be writing through your life, as I shared the story God was writing through mine. Sounds like a neat resource, right? So why isn't it available?

---

**Sometimes, it feels as though the story God is writing on our hearts has come to an end, but really, it's just a pause marked by a divinely placed comma.**

---

That pause may feel so long that you actually think it's the end of the story.

But it is not. Because. God. Is. Not. Yet. Done.

Sometimes it's hard to recognize how God is working His purposes in and through our stories. Sometimes we see a side of His work and presume that He must have written the last sentence.

For example, when I wrote *StoryHearts*, I thought God was done with the story. At that time, only a few months had passed since reconciling with my dad after four years of silence following a terrible falling out. After the process of forgiveness God walked me through, I thought I was healed and the story was finished, but God needed to do more work in my story heart. I thought the restoration of our relationship was the end of the story, but it turned out it was only the beginning.

I could write a book about what God has accomplished since the moment we reunited—but I know that it's not yet time. God is not yet done. And I don't want to try to get ahead of Him this time, even though I like to jump to the last chapter before starting the first. Is this your struggle too?

I confess I want to know the ending before I agree to the beginning. I want to know the outcome before I endure the waiting. But it's the journey that matters most.

---

## It's the unknowing in which we experience the gift of faith, as He writes His story for His glory.

---

It's in the waiting that we experience the blessing of God's provisions and the powerful sanctifying and transforming work He wants to accomplish in our lives.

I've come to believe that it's actually not the end of the story God wants us to be preoccupied with, as He's already told us what happens. Victory in Jesus. Eternity with our Creator. A forever home without tears or pain or loss.

It is actually in the present story He wants us to pursue Him most.

It is in the "no where" that God is actually "now here" … writing His story for His glory.

So will we embrace His story, even if the next chapter feels so uncertain, so far away?

## Cultivate

What story has God been writing in your heart? Where do you need to give Him greater access and time to accomplish His work for His glory?

# 25

I will love others without fear of rejection as His love overflows through me.

*For God has not given us a spirit of fear and timidity,*
*but of power, love, and self-discipline.*
2 TIMOTHY 1:7

*And may the Lord make your love for one another and for*
*all people grow and overflow, just as our love for you overflows.*
1 THESSALONIANS 3:12

*Such love has no fear, because perfect love expels all fear.*
*If we are afraid, it is for fear of punishment, and this shows*
*that we have not fully experienced his perfect love.*
1 JOHN 4:18

*Connect*

Father God, thank you for not giving us a spirit of fear and timidity, but of power, love, and self-discipline. Lord, please help us to love one another. May Your love grow within us so that it overflows from our hearts.

---

**Lord, we know that Your love has no fear because Your perfect love expels all fear.**

---

Take the fear we have stored up within our hearts and minds and replace it with the truth.

God, give us courage and the desire to love well.

May we press on in loving others, having experienced Your perfect love first.

In the strong name of Jesus, Amen.

# Consider

Do you find it easy to love others? Is it natural for you to respond in a loving way toward those God has placed in your life? When you see a practical need, are you quick to meet it? When someone wants to confide in you, do you listen attentively and respond with compassion? How do you react if you're asked to adjust your schedule to respond to a need of a friend or family member?

I struggle to love well. It may not look that way on the outside, but the reality is that within my heart and mind there is a constant battle. My flesh is constantly duking it out with the Spirit. Sometimes due to sheer laziness, as I'd rather sit with my feet up, then get off my duff to help a loved one out. Sometimes because I may feel like I'm being manipulated or taken advantage of. And sometimes, because I'm simply afraid of getting hurt if I put my heart on the line. Can you relate?

---

## Selfishness, laziness, and fear can not coexist with authentic loving-kindness.

---

To love well, we have to stop thinking of only ourselves.

To love well, we have to be passionate about being more like Jesus, choosing to become His hands and feet in every situation.

To love well, we have to be generous with our time and resources, reminding ourselves that God is our provider.

To love well, we have to stop being afraid of getting hurt.

To love well, we have to trust God to be the protector of our hearts.

To love well, we have to live with an overflowing mind-set, recognizing that it is God flowing through us that enables us to love well.

It's His love that we all need most. And it's His love that will win the battle between our spirit and flesh.

## Cultivate

How is God working in your life? How can you serve others through the overflow of what God is doing in you?

# 26

I will fear God and not seek the approval of any man or woman.

*Fear the Lord, you his holy people,*
*for those who fear him lack nothing.*
PSALM 34:9

*Do not be afraid of those who kill the body but cannot kill the soul.*
*Rather, be afraid of the One who can destroy both soul and body in hell.*
MATTHEW 10:28

*Am I now trying to win the approval of human beings,*
*or of God? Or am I trying to please people? If I were still*
*trying to please people, I would not be a servant of Christ.*
GALATIANS 1:10

# Connect

Father God, thank you that we do not have to live in fear. Thank you that we can trust You to protect us. Thank you for reminding us through Your Word to fear You alone as we work out our salvation with fear and trembling.

Thank you that we do not need to worry about seeking the approval of those we do life with, live with, work with, and serve.

We do not need to live in fear of rejection because You have already accepted us as Your beloved children.

---

**Lord, forgive us when our focus shifts to "what will they think" instead of "what will God think."**

---

Give us the desire in our inmost being to seek Your approval alone.

Give us a sense of awe about who You are so that the only fear that lives in us is truly a reverence for You.

In the strong name of Jesus, Amen.

# *Consider*

Do you struggle with wanting to be liked? Oh, I know that sounds so petty, like ten-year-old girls on the playground at school. But I don't think we ever outgrow the desire to be embraced by our peers and those we do life with. We simply discover that "being liked" doesn't change our value.

---

**Being popular doesn't make us more important, even if our inner little girl begs to differ.**

---

Maybe you don't care so much about being included by the in-crowd or being noticed by those who you think matter most. Maybe your struggle is more like mine, where your longing for approval is really about a fear of rejection. While I am totally fine with being "un-noticed," I worry about being criticized and misunderstood. Can you relate? I've learned to live without positive feedback. I can survive being overlooked in a large crowd. But verbal criticism causes me to just crumble. Does it do that to you too?

When it comes to relationships, where love binds us together, I can handle it a little better. I'll cry. Maybe pitch a defensive fit. Then "come to" and walk in humility to solve the problem. But what about those "not in real life" rejections? The kind we find in today's social media world of un-likers, un-followers, and un-subscribers.

Does this kind of passive rejection stab your heart, revealing your longing to be liked?

I've actually gotten used to the whole drama of likes and unlikes, but it's the hurtful email filled with accusations from a stranger (yes, that happens often), which manages to rock my world. Kind of stupid, don't you think? Why should I allow a stranger that kind of power over my sense of worth? Because I get caught in the approval trap, fearing people more than God. And that, my friend, is a problem. Is it one you struggle with too? Well, then maybe this strategy might work for you.

When I find myself feel disapproved by people, I turn to the Lord with these two questions:

1. Does their criticism have any merit that I ought to heed, or were their words from the overflow of their own wounds?
2. If I am living to seek Your approval only, God, what is the response and next steps You'd have me take?

Responding to fear and rejection requires honest communication with God. Plain and simple.

He'll show us the truth if we're willing to ask for it. He'll show us when the situation at hand is an opportunity for Him to do a deeper work in transforming us to become more like Christ. And He'll show us when we simply need to move forward in faith, dismissing the accusation, as we seek Him for the courage to move through the fear of further rejection. Living for the approval of God alone really does begin with turning our ears and eyes toward Him.

## Cultivate

How do you face your fears and times of rejection? Is there a different approach God wants you to take?

# 27

I will be thankful to God
in all circumstances.

*Be thankful in all circumstances, for this is*
*God's will for you who belong to Christ Jesus.*
1 THESSALONIANS 5:18

# Connect

Father, thank you for asking us to do what is already good for us, like choosing to be thankful in all things. It's amazing how such a simple little instruction can matter so much, and yet be so hard to put into action.

---

## Lord, infuse our hearts with thankfulness.

---

Root out in us a spirit of discontentment and grumbling. Convict us of an attitude of jealousy when we should choose gratitude.

Move us into a posture of thankfulness that we may glorify You with our words and deeds.

In the strong name of Jesus, Amen.

# Consider

Have you ever considered the correlation between gratitude and joy? How about complaining and misery? What about an attitude of thankfulness and hope compared to an endless critical commentary that leads to an overwhelming sense of despair?

---

## How we feel dictates how we live.

---

Maybe that's why God calls us to be thankful in all circumstances because He knows that a posture of thankfulness leads to a life that is abundantly more joyful and impactful. Did you know that a person who is grateful and kind actually has a healthier brain map? So, should we be surprised that the Designer of our bodies has already told us to do what is good for us?

Think about it this way: Who would you identify as life-givers in your family, among your friends, or at your place of work or ministry? What is it about them that makes being around them so easy? How about those people who are life drainers? What do you feel as you anticipate time together?

Okay, now let's get personal: Which camp do you fall into? Are you a life-giver, full of gratitude, thankfulness, and overflowing hope? Or are you a life-drainer with a never-ending stream of complaints, making you and everyone else miserable as you despair about life?

Maybe you fall somewhere in between depending on the day and hour. I confess I can easily swing from gratitude to grumbling. I like to blame it on the fact that I feel so deeply. I can be passionately filled with joy one minute and easily consumed by negativity the next. But here's the deal, regardless of what we feel, being thankful is a matter of obedience.

God tells us plain and simple, be thankful.

So why do we resist doing so, especially when such blessings are in store for us? Because we are a stubborn and rebellious people, just like the Israelites (read Psalm 78 to get an overview). Not much has changed in us over all these years inhabiting the earth.

What God said was good for His people back then is still just as important today.

So will we learn from the generations that have gone before us? Or will we grumble at every turn? Will we follow in their footsteps, with stubborn, rebellious hearts? Or will we finally submit to doing what God says is best?

## Cultivate

What is one practical step you can take toward developing a consistent attitude of gratitude?

# 28

I will be teachable and seek
wisdom from godly counsel.

*Tune your ears to wisdom, and concentrate on understanding.*
PROVERBS 2:2

*If you listen to constructive criticism,*
*you will be at home among the wise.*
PROVERBS 15:31

*If you need wisdom, ask our generous God, and he will*
*give it to you. He will not rebuke you for asking.*
JAMES 1:5

# Connect

Lord God, Your kindness is beyond words. We are so thankful that You are willing to take our selfish hearts and teach us godliness.

God, thank you for being approachable and urging us to seek wisdom from You.

Forgive us when we turn elsewhere in search of answers, instead of pursuing truth and guidance from Your Word.

---

**God, please tune our ears to wisdom and give us a desire to not only understand it but to apply it.**

---

Keep us humble, God, that we may respond well to constructive criticism and respond with a teachable heart to those who have biblical wisdom to impart upon us.

In the strong name of Jesus, Amen.

# *Consider*

When you find yourself in the kind of situation that requires a clear-cut decision, how do you go about deciding what to do? I'm not referring to whether you're going to order a pizza with pepperoni or mushrooms, but rather the kind of decision that will impact your future and those you do life with.

Are you impulsive? Do you delay making a decision because you're afraid of the potentially wrong consequences? Do you seek out the counsel of the wise or the opinion of the world? Do you often struggle with feeling like you simply don't have enough information to make a decision?

As a life coach, you might count me as an expert in helping people make decisions since one of the main reasons people come for coaching is that they feel stuck and are uncertain as to what to do next. I've witnessed clients struggle in moving forward because they are big idea girls and can't parse through all their creativity to find an answer.

For some, it's a personality issue, some people always feel like they need more information.

For others, it's a past-trauma issue, as they fear getting hurt again and have an unhealthy desire to please others. And for some, it's simply a matter of lack of margin space in an information overloaded world. Of course, there are a bazillion other reasons why we may feel stuck when it comes to making a decision.

---

**What's so interesting about coaching, however, is that I don't tell people what to do, because advice never works.**

---

For example, when was the last time you heard a great sermon, but failed to put into action what the pastor said? What about when you sought out advice from a friend or parent? Did you do what they said to do? Are you indeed teachable?

---

## We need to own the "ah-ha" moment in order to carry out the solution.

---

But if that's true, what's the point of listening to a sermon in the first place? And why bother seeking out the counsel of the wise? Or even hiring a life coach?

Because there is value in embracing wisdom, expressing our struggles, and engaging in the pursuit of a godly solution.

*Embracing:*
We need to embrace the wisdom found in the Word and the wise counsel of godly women. This will enable the Holy Spirit to lead us in the right direction.

*Expressing:*
We need to articulate our struggle in making a decision, both to the Lord and to those who offer trustworthy counsel, because in expressing ourselves, we get to own our thought process, pinpoint our fears, and brainstorm solutions.

*Engaging:*
Accountability and encouragement come from sharing our struggles and the steps we plan to take moving forward so that we can stay the course.

God has the solutions for us. He is the one who enables us to sift through all the emotions to get down to the truth as it is found in His Word. That's why one of the questions I use the most with clients is: "What do you think God has to say about this?"

There's no better option than asking the Word Himself to speak and orchestrate the solution for every situation.

When we seek God for wisdom, we can move forward with confidence that He will give it to us generously.

## Cultivate

What will be your go-to response next time you face a situation in which you have to make a decision?

# 29

I will honor others because they are made in the image of God.

*So God created human beings in his own image.*
*In the image of God he created them;*
*male and female he created them.*
GENESIS 1:27 NIV

*Love each other with genuine affection,*
*and take delight in honoring each other.*
ROMANS 12:10 NIV

# Connect

God, it is hard to believe You made us in Your own image. If we let that soak into our minds, how would that change the way we treat those we're in a relationship with and interact with each day?

Might we be more thoughtful about our words? Would we think twice about that off-the-cuff comment or unnecessary critique? Would we put aside our own needs and choose to serve, even though it's uncomfortable?

---

## God, forgive us for not showing genuine affection to those You've called us to love.

---

Forgive us for not taking delight in honoring the men and women made in Your image.

Transform our thinking about honor so that our actions and words might be in line with Your Word and call.

In the strong name of Jesus, Amen.

# *Consider*

What do you think it means to honor others, especially because they are made in the image of God?

I really hadn't considered the concept of biblical honor until attending an assembly at my children's elementary school years ago. The principal took the microphone and explained to the children what honor looks like in the context of school life. He described honor as telling the truth and obeying the teacher, listening attentively to peers and not making fun of one another. I found my thoughts rewinding to my own childhood, wondering what would have happened if honor had been the driving force not only in my school experience but especially in my family.

Wouldn't you agree that there's really no place for screaming and yelling or the silent treatment and eye rolling in a relationship that is defined by honor?

Choosing to honor each other sets the tone and parameters for communicating in a respectful, thoughtful, healthy, and holy way.

---

**For honor to become a priority, we have to believe it's not just a good idea but rather it's a command God expects us to obey.**

---

We choose to honor one another in submission to His will. And we choose to honor one another because we're made in His image.

Believing that truth actually changes everything. For example, my daughter faced one of the most difficult decisions of her life after stumbling upon social media bullying by her school mates. As a leader in her school, she felt it was her duty to respond. But it was the deepest part of her convictions that motivated her actions. She felt her peers crossed a line, because, in her words, "I don't care whether they don't like her. She is the *Imageo Deo*, and because of that, her life has value."

Yes, all those years of Latin along with a handful of great Bible teachers and the work of the Holy Spirit opened my daughter's eyes to the unchangeable truth that we are indeed made in the image of God. Because of that, she couldn't stand by. Because of that, she had to find a way to bring honor back to a classmate who wasn't even her friend.

There is a reason God calls us to remember that we are made in His image and urges us to love each other with genuine affection, taking delight in honoring one another—it's because it is simply not in our nature. In our flesh, we are more prone to wounding one another than acting kindly, respectfully, and lovingly. But by His grace, we can beg the Spirit to override our nature so that we can embrace the call to treat all with honor for the glory of God.

## Cultivate

Is it a struggle to treat others with honor? How could you move in this direction by keeping at the forefront of your mind the *Imageo Deo*—that we are made in the image of our Creator?

# 30

I will respect the men in my life
and not belittle or degrade them.

*So again I say, each man must love his wife as he
loves himself, and the wife must respect her husband.*
EPHESIANS 5:33

*Never speak harshly to an older man, but appeal to
him respectfully as you would to your own father.
Talk to younger men as you would to your own brothers.*
1 TIMOTHY 5:1

# Connect

God, thank you for providing us with even the simplest of instructions regarding relationships. You don't leave us to figure it out on our own, although that's what we often choose to do. Please forgive us for neglecting Your truth and in turn, causing ourselves and others harm.

Lord, it can be so hard to speak and act respectfully toward the men in our lives, especially if we have not been treated in a way that is respectable.

---

**God, help us find healing and the power to forgive, while we boldly strive to abide by Your instructions.**

---

Lord, please motivate us to honor biblical marriage. For those of us who are wives, I pray You give us the desire to understand what respecting our husbands looks like from Your perspective. For those of us who are moms, please enable us to communicate respect to our sons and teach our daughters how to follow suit.

Give us a sensitivity in our spirits so that our words and actions communicate a respect rooted in the fact that the men in our lives are made in Your image.

Open our ears to hear what disrespect sounds like. Open our eyes to see the impact of our disrespectful treatment of the men in our lives. Guard our tongues against speaking in disrespectful ways. All for Your glory, God.

In the strong name of Jesus, Amen.

# Consider

How would you respond if your mother-in-law handed you a book titled *Proper Care and Feeding of Husbands*? Yes, that was my experience, and as you might imagine, it was hard to not feel judged! Was I not doing a good job at being a godly wife to my husband? By the time I got through chapter one, I shockingly discovered the answer to that question for myself. I was sabotaging my marriage because of the way I was disrespectfully treating my husband.

I was nagging, critical, controlling, and condescending, but I had no idea until I saw myself in the stories in that book! I was completely unaware how the culturally pervasive attitude that "all men are stupid" oozed through the tone in my voice. From a biblical perspective, you could easily categorize me as "that quarrelsome wife" consumed by worldly standards (Proverbs 21:9). I treated my husband more like a son, mothering him in every aspect of our life together.

But by the grace of God, He opened my eyes to see the implications of my behavior. Through the teachings of Dr. Emmerson Eggerich, especially in his video series, "Love and Respect," I came to see how my tone of voice and choice of words were utterly disrespectful and crushing to my husband. The first step was for me to apologize to my husband, and the second was to learn a new way of communicating not only with my husband but also with my son. Yes, both need to hear respect!

Together, my husband and I spent an entire summer working through the "Love and Respect" video teaching series, which I'm convinced is what God used to save our marriage. I discovered not only my husband's need for respect, but also my need for love, and the way our choice of words and actions will either nurture intimacy and connection or drive us apart.

A lack of respect is how a marriage begins to crumble. But wouldn't you agree that most of us think that a lack of love is the problem? It's actually not the root issue. The breakdown in respect manifests itself in what we eventually see in emotional affairs, adultery, addictions, pornography, financial discord, and more.

> **Respect has nothing at all to do with what we feel is deserved and earned. It's what we give in submission to the Word and out of reverence for Christ.**

Ephesians 5:11-21 describes the daunting responsibilities for a husband to follow the example of Christ in caring for his bride, so one might naturally think respect is earned. But that's not the command Paul gives. He simply says, "And the wife must respect her husband." He doesn't say, "must respect her husband if ...."

So how do we, as women, demonstrate respect to our husbands and the men in our lives?

Respect begins with tone and humility as we treat the men in our lives in light of the truth that they are made in the image of God.

We need to be quick to ask, "Did that offend you? Did I disrespect you by what I just said? I'm sorry." And we need to be equally guarded against sarcastic, sexists, and groupist comments. Yes, we women can be guilty of "all men are" accusations, feeding into the mentality that women are smarter, better, and "more than" the men in our lives. It's also about making a place for the men in our lives to be men—and mamas, that starts when they are boys.

It's not about whether men deserve respect. It's about giving respect as we yield to the Word and submit to the call put on us by God.

## Cultivate

In what ways have you not been respectful to the men in your life? What will you do to change that from this point forward?

# 31

I will not make an idol of anyone
(especially a spouse or child) or anything
(project, title, degree, accomplishment).

*So be careful not to break the covenant*
*the Lord your God has made with you.*
*Do not make idols of any shape or form,*
*for the Lord your God has forbidden this.*
DEUTERONOMY 4:23

*They exchanged the truth about God for a lie,*
*and worshiped and served created things rather than*
*the Creator—who is forever praised. Amen.*
ROMANS 1:25

# Connect

God, thank you for the covenant of love that You've made with us, which is for our good. Forgive us for the ways we do not hold up our end, as we make idols in any and every shape, even though You've told us not to do so.

Oh Lord, we're so clueless about the ways we make idols in our modern-day world. Forgive us!

Really, nothing has changed since the moment You spun the world into being and made us in Your image.

How easily we exchange the truth about You for a lie.

We worship and serve our created things and even the things You've created, instead of You, our Creator.

Forgive us for doing this unknowingly.

**Open our eyes to see more clearly, so that we may change our ways and crush the stronghold of idolatry through the power of the Holy Spirit and in the name of Jesus.**

In the strong name of Jesus, Amen.

# Consider

What do you think a modern-day idol looks like? Are you imagining turning a corner and coming upon a golden calf? Or do you think of idolatry more in the form of a kind of worship for those who are not Christ-followers?

---

## Idolatry is simply the worship of anyone or anything more than God.

---

Honestly, I didn't know I had an idolatry issue until I stumbled upon a sermon series years ago. I was so shocked and alarmed at the reality God was revealing to me. How could I, a Bible-believing Christian be caught in the snare of idolatry? Maybe you're wondering the same.

At face value, it might be hard to discern if idolatry is a sin issue for you. I'd hedge a bet it is because I've never met a person who doesn't struggle in the worship of someone or something other than God. But the way that it will manifest itself in each of our lives is different. For me, my issue of idolatry is around productivity. It's more important to me to "get 'er done" than to consider the needs of those I'm called to love well and serve authentically. Can you relate?

My finished "to-do" list full of creative projects is indeed my idol because it robs time from worshipping God and heeding His commands to enjoy rest and fellowship. Feeling good about what I've finished is more important than pleasing the God who made my hands and mind and heart to serve Him. At least, that's how it was until I came to see the root sin of idolatry. Since then, I've learned how to walk the tender road of confession and repentance, asking God to change the motives of my heart.

There is a litmus test to figure out if you're trapped in idolatry. The clue is your reaction when that "thing" or "person" is messed with.

What do I mean "messed with"? Well, what's the irritation level in your soul if you have to let go of that thing you've set your heart and mind on to focus on the needs of someone or something else?

*If work is your idol, how do you react when you need to "leave early" to tend to a family matter?*

*If your family is your idol, how do you handle life when your family members aren't conforming to your expectations for how they ought to treat you or behave?*

*If your children are your idol, how do you react toward God at the threat of a health crisis or life-altering event that could harm them forever?*

*If your house is your idol, how do you respond to your family when they make a mess of it?*

*If material things are your idol, how do you handle matters when you don't have the finances to buy that thing you want right now?*

*If fitness is your idol, what is your attitude when you can't work out?*

*If time is your idol, what do you do when someone requires something of you that interrupts your schedule?*

*If your reputation is your idol, how do you respond to being misunderstood?*

*If your credentials are your idol, how many more degrees and certifications do you need in order to be good enough?*

*If being liked is your idol, how much more do you need to do to get more followers?*

In other words, when God doesn't conform life to your plans, desires, and expectations, how do you respond? Are you spitting mad or able to surrender to His purposes?

If our heart's cry is "Only, You God!," we're in a position to battle again the pull of idolatry.

It's when we give up that singular focus that we find ourselves at the doorway to idolatry and one step away from sin. But the good news is that in Christ we've been given the opportunity to seek God's forgiveness, move forward in repentance, and experience total transformation as we yield our desires to the Lord's leading.

## Cultivate

How do you think this matter of idolatry has impacted your relationship with God and others? What step do you need to take with the Lord to tackle the thing that tempts you to make it into an idol?

# 32

I will continue to ask God to enable
me to live a life worthy of His call with
the power to accomplish all things
as my faith prompts me to do.

*So we keep on praying for you, asking our
God to enable you to live a life worthy of his call.
May he give you the power to accomplish
all the good things your faith prompts you to do.*
2 THESSALONIANS 1:11

# *Connect*

God, we are so grateful that You don't ask us to operate in our own power or strength. Thank you, Lord, for filling us with Your presence through Jesus Christ and leading us through the working of the Holy Spirit.

Forgive us when we go about pursuing our own plans and taking matters into our own hands.

Forgive us for not praying about everything and anything.

Forgive us when we run from the call You've given us … a worthy call to live a life of joining You in Your work and giving You all the glory!

---

**Lord, we ask You to prompt us in faith to accomplish everything for Your glory and purpose.**

---

In the strong name of Jesus, Amen.

## *Consider*

How do you respond to an obstacle or rerouting of your plans? Let's say you had a particular idea in mind for what the summer was supposed to look like, but every day delivered a need or interruption that wrecked your schedule. Or what if the circumstances that arise out of the blue are totally outside of your control, like a health or financial crisis, a betrayal in a relationship or simply the falling out of a friendship with no explanation at all? How do you respond?

Life happens, and we're forced to respond.

Maybe you've figured this out already, but we're not actually in control of our circumstances even though we're expected to make wise choices moment by moment. We may set upon a course, only to have it not conform to our desires. We invest in others, but without the promise of return. We go about our business, only to discover there's a greater need before us requiring our attention. And then we're cranky, irritable, and downright difficult to be around because our lives don't match our plans.

---

## What if our plans and pursuits were prompted by our faith?

---

What if prayer came first, leading us to join God in the worthy call He places on our lives?

Instead of striving toward our own agenda, what would it look like to submit to the one the Lord has for us? Yes, we can go about making our plans, but what if those plans were prayed over, around, and through before we took action?

Would our actions then be prompted by faith as we respond to the worthy call God has placed on our lives?

Could it be that His worthy call for us may look like walking through a trial instead of skirting around it? Might a worthy call require an interruption in our work day to meet a practical need for our sister in Christ? What if His call is to put aside our aspirations to put on the mind of Christ and God's kingdom purposes?

Come to think of it—when the phone rings, it's always an interruption. We get to choose to take that call, not knowing what we'll hear or what will be requested of us. Should we be surprised that God's call on our life functions in the same way? So, will we answer, quickly hang up before saying hello, or send God straight to voicemail?

## *Cultivate*

How is God seeking to get your attention so that you might answer the worthy call He has for your life—one that is prompted by faith and led by prayer?

# 33

I will seek God daily for a deeper understanding of His word.

*Make them holy by your truth;*
*teach them your word, which is truth.*
JOHN 17:17

*For the word of God is alive and powerful.*
*It is sharper than the sharpest two-edged sword,*
*cutting between soul and spirit, between joint and*
*marrow. It exposes our innermost thoughts and desires.*
HEBREWS 4:12 NIV

# Connect

God, thank you for Your Word, which is truly a gift to us and a source of truth that we can count on. Thank you that Your truth makes us holy.

Yes, Lord, we believe that Your Word is alive and powerful, sharper than the sharpest two-edged sword, cutting between soul and spirit, joint and marrow.

---

## Your Word exposes our innermost thoughts and desires.

---

God, thank you that Your Word brings into the light secrets forged in darkness.

It sets us free. It heals. It reminds us of Your promises. It reveals the places of Your provision.

Forgive us when we discount Your Word as truth.

Forgive us when we neglect reading Your Word. Motivate us to make our time in Scripture the first priority each day.

In the strong name of Jesus, Amen.

# *Consider*

What is your definition of truth? According to dictionary.com, truth is "the true or actual state of a matter, conformity with fact or reality; verity; a verified or indisputable fact, proposition, principle; the state or character of being true."

But how do you verify truth? How do you prove it as indisputable? Is truth something you simply have to accept by faith? But is that an oxymoron, since faith is a choice to believe what cannot be proven?

---

**By faith we believe what we can't see and embrace as truth what we cannot prove.**

---

Isn't that what is required of us when we accept the Word as a "verified or indisputable fact"? Or do we only believe what we see and understand? If that's the case, it's not truth we're after but comfortability. We're living by feelings and are guided by moral or cultural norms.

Sometimes, it takes being removed from all that is familiar to see truth afresh.

I remember that moment in my London dorm room when I placed my faith in Jesus Christ as Lord. I chose to risk my own understanding for how I thought God worked in favor of believing the promise of salvation explained by my friend. I didn't yet have the Word in my hand, but I trusted that her understanding of Scripture was worth heeding.

More than two decades later, I'm so glad I did, because the Holy Spirit has faithfully opened up my heart and mind to see the truth as I read God's Word for myself and saw evidence of His promises in my life.

How? Well, there's not a passage of Scripture that doesn't describe the struggles I've faced and strongholds I have overcome. Have you found the same to be true?

God's Word causes us to consider our actions honestly and thoughts purposefully.

We become accountable to our habits and choices, reactions and responses, as the Holy Spirit leads and convicts us to turn from our sin and into the freedom found in Christ. That dance is really a spiritual sword fight as the Word is wielded like a double-edged sword, cutting through every part of us—every thought, decision, and action—to remove from our lives sin and strongholds and bring forth what is holy, right, and pure.

## Cultivate

What would a bystander say about the way you're living your life? Is there evidence that you are living according to the truth as found in the Word of God?

# 34

I will strive to be filled
up by Jesus Christ, the
Living Water, and not others.

*Jesus answered her, "If you knew the gift of God and
who it is that asks you for a drink, you would have asked
him and he would have given you living water."*
JOHN 4:10

*Whoever believes in me, as Scripture has said,
rivers of living water will flow from within them.*
JOHN 7:38

# *Connect*

God, thank you for providing us with a kind of refreshment and filling that we cannot find anywhere else.

---

**Thank you, God, that all we have to do is ask You for what we need, and You promise to provide.**

---

We don't have to jump through spiritual hoops. We don't have to do anything to prove our worth to You. We simply need to come to You, as we are, and trust You to care for our souls, our hearts, our minds, our bodies, and our needs.

Give us eyes to see Your provisions, especially when what we ask for looks different from what You deliver.

God, we do want the gift of Living Water most of all. We want Jesus to flow through us and fill us up. Please root out anything that is standing in the way. Please show us our sin, bitterness, greed, selfishness, impure motives, and unforgiveness, that we may repent and be forgiven by You, thus making room for Jesus to dwell more fully in our lives. Please show us the idols we make of people and things, settling for false Gods instead of You. May nothing and no one else separate us from You.

May we find our complete satisfaction in You, the Living Water.

In the strong name of Jesus, Amen.

# Consider

Where do you go to get filled up? How do you tend to that ache in your soul? That longing for approval? Who has turned into your mini-savior? To take from you the pain in your heart? To carry a load that feels too heavy to bear up for even one more step?

It's so easy to turn to that in-the-flesh friend or spouse or coworker or even child to meet a need that only the cross can satisfy.

On the one hand, we are supposed to lean into those we're doing life with within the body of Christ. They are our family. We are knit together and meant to serve one another. But wouldn't you agree that there is this fine line between serving and sucking one another dry?

Yes, we need to be there for each other. But we also need to be quick to own our limitations and admit our need for the Savior who can satisfy our souls with a kind of refreshment that isn't found anywhere else.

---

**We all have this deep need to be filled up by Jesus Himself, and yet we run to everyone else instead.**

---

But why? I happen to think the reason is the same for us as it was for the Samaritan woman. Jesus stood before her, offering to fill her life to the brim with the fullness of Himself, the Living Water. Can you think of anything more satisfying? But she didn't recognize this gift because she was too focused on herself. I'm not saying she was narcissistic but rather consumed with an identity shaped by her sin and past.

She couldn't shake off "what was" to embrace "what is."

Jesus stood before her, seeing a woman made in the image of God. He knew her sin, but He also knew that wasn't her identity. It was her behavior, not her worth.

Her past was not a predictor for her future.

The Son of God, the Messiah, the Redeemer and Savior and Rescuerer of Souls offered her life by faith through grace, not works.

Doesn't He do the same for us? Jesus pours out Himself, the Living Water, to wash us clean and fill our lives with a love that can penetrate into every nook and cranny of our hearts and minds. His love changes us. His presence refuels us. His work in our lives transforms us. So will we receive what He has to offer us—Living Water to satisfy our parched and weary souls from now until eternity?

## Cultivate

How are you turning to everyone else instead of Jesus for a soul-filling satisfaction? What does it look like to turn to Jesus and receive what He has to offer you?

# 35

I will remember that God gives life
to the full, the abundant life, but the
enemy comes to steal, kill, and destroy.

*The thief comes only to steal and kill and destroy.*
*I came that they may have life and have it abundantly.*
JOHN 10:10 ESV

## Connect

God, we are so grateful that Your Word provides us with truth we can build our lives upon. You don't give us false hope. You don't promise a life without pain or heartache, without trials or challenges.

In fact, You tell us to be prepared and careful, to be on guard and discerning, for there is a thief that comes only to steal and kill and destroy us.

God, there is no one who has not experienced Satan's handiwork. We know his persecution. We know his attacks. We know his deceiving and cunning work. But we also have the privilege of knowing You and Your mighty, fierce, merciful, and loving hand.

---

**God, thank you that we get to experience Your remarkable power and provisions through faith in Jesus Christ, our Savior, who secures for us a full and abundant life.**

---

Thank you for this gift.
In the strong name of Jesus, Amen.

# *Consider*

Can you pinpoint where the enemy had a field day messing with you and those you love? Did he go after your identity or security? Did he attack your family, marriage, or children? Was he busy stealing joy and instilling fear in the everyday mundane moments? What antics did he display in your workplace or church community?

Satan is busy, always. He's about the business of tormenting God's children.

So it should be no surprise that his handiwork is woven throughout our life story. So maybe, the more pressing question isn't "What did Satan do to you, but how did you respond?"

Did you fight back with your sword in hand, using the Word of God as the weapon to defeat the enemy? Did you invite your brothers and sisters in Christ to circle around you to pray for healing, victory, freedom? Or were you crushed and defeated, feeling abandoned by God?

---

**We will be prepared to fight against the enemy's attempts to steal, kill, and destroy us, if we cling to God, His Word, and the fellowship of believers.**

---

But that's a lesson most of us seem to have to learn the hard way. At least, that's what it was like for me. There was one particular experience that proved to me the need to be on guard with the Word in hand, trusting God in my heart, and relying on the support of my sisters in Christ.

As I was preparing to travel across the country to give a weekend retreat on the topic of holiness, my husband came down with a bizarre virus and ended up on a mega-dose of antibiotics. He seemed healed enough for me to leave, and I expected to come home to a normal life.

But while I was gone, disaster ensued. Our beloved boarding school community ended up in a three-hour long staff meeting that ultimately divided and destroyed relationships. Meanwhile, I was gallivanting around San Francisco post-retreat and lost my cell phone. I borrowed my host's phone in an attempt to reach my husband, checking with him before buying a new phone, but couldn't reach him until after the stores closed because he was in the middle of that horrible meeting.

The next day I flew home and ended up stranded in the airport, unable to reach the car service or my husband for hours, because I had no phone. I ended up borrowing phones from strangers, but no one answered. Bizarre, I know. But by the grace of God, I found another car service to take me home. I got home at midnight, instead of 6 p.m., and I collapsed into my husband's arms, exhausted. The next day my husband woke up with a fever again and was hospitalized for the next five days as he fought for his life.

The next three months were simply a blur of survival … spiritual survival.

Instead of clinging to God, I withdrew.

I couldn't understand why so many "awful" things had to happen at the same time God was opening the door to ministry opportunities I had longed prayed for. The trial was so great I told God I didn't want to travel or speak anymore.

At the moment, I quit the dream and the calling because the cost was too high. Have you done the same?

It took years for me to recognize what the enemy had been up to—stealing the dream, killing my testimony, destroying the opportunity to spread the Good News. That's because I wasn't wise to his antics. I had been caught in a worldly mind-set that if I did everything right all should go well for me. And if it was hard, I should quit, because I don't do hard. Can you relate?

Satan played me well. Until I realized what he had been up to and what it had cost. I didn't want to throw away all that God had done in my life and the opportunity to share His Good News just because it was hard. I wanted to testify for the glory of God, in spite of the suffering. But in order to do so, I had to come to terms with the fact that the abundant life God offers us doesn't have anything to do with experiencing a carefree, easy, and happy-go-lucky life.

The abundantly full life God promises is what we experience in the depths of our soul when His presence dwells fully within us.

His abundance comes through His love infusing every nook and cranny of our lives.

His abundance comes through His hope overflowing in every situation, even the most difficult and dire ones.

His abundance comes through His grace and mercy touching every part of us in need of healing.

---

## The abundant life we crave is a life filled with His abundance.

---

It's not a life without trials, but rather it is the fullness of God sustaining us through them.

## Cultivate

How has God been with you, upholding you, during the times you've felt the enemy attacking you?

# 36

## I will learn to sit quietly to hear from God.

*Be still, and know that I am God!*
*I will be honored by every nation.*
*I will be honored throughout the world.*
PSALM 46:10

*Truly my soul finds rest in God;*
*my salvation comes from him.*
PSALM 62:1 NIV

*My sheep listen to my voice;*
*I know them, and they follow me.*
JOHN 10:27 NIV

# Connect

Thank you, Father, for being a God of rest. Thank you for being a God who sees us and wants to be seen by us. Oh Lord, this is so counter cultural!

God, You invite us to be still. To find our rest in You. To find security in our salvation. To be attentive to Your voice. To be known by You and know You. Yet how often we feel rushed, overlooked, and frazzled.

Please, Lord, forgive us for living in a way You didn't design and for making chaos our norm.

Forgive us for neglecting time with You. Please lead us in obedience to Your Word.

---

**Make us attentive to Your voice, God, and eliminate from our lives all that distracts us from living according to Your design.**

---

In the strong name of Jesus, Amen.

# *Consider*

How would you describe the state of your life right now? Are you embracing margin space? Finding time to sit with the Lord and hear His voice? Or are you in total chaos? Hurried? Distracted? Behind? Overwhelmed?

Do you feel like you just need to make it to _____? Is that date on the calendar the finish line of a looming deadline? The changing of seasons? What do you think life has for you when you finally make it to that point?

I happen to be breathing deeply in the grace and mercy of God once again. But all that transpired before getting to this point could be described as total chaos, as I was striving to meet a deadline while also taking on a project I was convinced the Lord had for me. All along, I wondered if the chaos could be the result of obedience to the Spirit's leading, especially since what I was working toward didn't end up how I expected.

From this vantage point, it looks like I took a detour rather than ending up at the destination point. Have you felt that way too?

There is, however, one blessing still unfolding. The unexpected result spurred me on into a time of soul searching and heart-deep investigating. As a result, I now have tremendous clarity and vision for not only my work but also for my personal life as well as an unexpected gift … margin space. Breathing room. Opportunities to go deeper and not just wider.

A clear and distinct "no" from God has turned into a "yes" to so much more.

More time for sitting long with the Lord. More time for fellowship with sweet friends. More time for following through on things like balancing our family budget and organizing the chaos in the basement. More time for tackling that long work to-do list. More time to hear from God.

More time, that is focused time, is indeed a gift from the Lord.

---

## A great big NO from God can actually be a blessing when it leads to stillness with Him.

---

Are you in a season where God is urging you to be still and know, once again, that He is God? Is He providing a place for your soul to rest? Is He creating a stillness in your life and quietness in your thoughts so that you can more clearly hear His voice? Oh friend, that sound is so, so, so sweet—much sweet than chaos and hurry and accomplishing anything this side of heaven.

*Cultivate*

How might God be using the limits He's placed on you to create space for you to know Him, rest in Him, and hear from Him?

# 37

I will devote time to pray for those God has brought into my life and the needs He lays on my heart.

*Keep watch and pray, so that you will not give in to temptation. For the spirit is willing, but the body is weak!*
MATTHEW 26:41 NIV

*Night and day we pray earnestly for you, asking God to let us see you again to fill the gaps in your faith.*
1 THESSALONIANS 3:10

*Never stop praying.*
1 THESSALONIANS 5:17

## Connect

Thank you, God, that You invite us to participate in Your kingdom work through prayer. Thank you for the reminder that we are to keep watch and pray as a way to resist the temptations that will come our way. You don't leave us defenseless. You give us a way out before we even find ourselves trapped in the enemy's snares.

God, You know our spirit is willing, but our body is weak. Please strengthen us and uphold us with Your righteous right hand. Use us to intercede on behalf of our brothers and sisters in Christ, that together we may find our strength in You.

---

**God, remind us daily of the
calling and privilege to devote
our hearts and minds to prayer.**

---

May we be earnest in our prayers and not simply checking off a spiritual "to-do" list. God, give us the determination and desire to never stop praying for the needs You allow us to see and feel.

In the strong name of Jesus, Amen.

# Consider

How would you describe your prayer life? Do you find yourself only praying "on the go," lifting up your needs to the Lord moment by moment? Or do you find that praying requires quiet in order to concentrate and focus your heart on connecting with God?

Have you ever thought about how many factors are at play when it comes to cultivating a robust prayer life?

Our schedules can make or break it, right? The demands upon us can drive us to prayer or steal our attention away. Have you ever considered how our personalities, especially in regards to our communication style, can also impact the way our prayer life looks? Chatty Cathy's won't have nearly as much trouble talking with God compared to those whose words are few and far between.

The kind of communication style seen in our most intimate relationships is likely reflected in our prayer life, too.

You might guess that I'm a words girl, whether I'm writing or talking, and so I not only have a lot to say to my husband but also to God. When it comes to my prayer life, I have journals filled with my thoughts and requests. But the question is, how am I doing at listening to the Lord and sitting long enough to hear His still small voice? Can you relate?

My husband, on the other hand, speaks only when necessary. He simply doesn't feel like much needs to be said. He's not filled more than one page in one journal in all our years together, but that's not evidence of his lack of a prayer life. Does he struggle at times to express himself to the Lord? Yes, but does that mean his prayer life doesn't exist? Not at all.

---

**When it comes to evaluating our prayer life, the worst thing we can do is compare ourselves.**

---

Prayer is about connecting with God in the exact way He made each of us.

*It's not about the number of words we use or don't use.*
*It is about using the words we have to lift up to the Lord the needs we see.*

*It's not about using a journal or illustrating a Bible.*
*It is about taking the time to speak to God about those we're called to love ... our friends and family and enemies, too.*

*It's not about making lists or following a formula.*
*It is about paying attention to what God says to talk to Him about, like temptation and fear and worry.*

*It's not about getting what we want, simply because we ask.*
*It is about yielding our hearts and minds and desires to the Lord, seeking His will to be done.*

Prayer isn't simply us rambling on to the Lord. It isn't about asking for what we need so that life goes a little bit easier. Prayer is about slowing our lives down to lay our requests before the God of the universe while seeking His will for His kingdom here on earth. God has a voice as much as we do, so prayer should be about hearing Him as much as it is about us speaking up about our needs.

Prayer is really a matter of connecting with God in an open and honest two-way conversation.

Prayer is also about co-laboring with Him in His plans as we intercede on behalf of His children. It's about confessing our sin and getting right with Him. It's about receiving His forgiveness and responding with humility and gratitude. It's about praising God for who He is and what He has done, even if it doesn't turn out how we expected.

Being devoted to prayer isn't simply a good idea, it's a necessary step of faith out of obedience to the Lord's instructions. He tells us to pray and also what to pray for, so it's not like we have an "out." Regardless of our communication style, we are to be a people of prayer. And in taking up this call, we not only draw closer to Him but also participate in His kingdom work.

## Cultivate

What steps can you take this week to become a woman devoted to prayer?

# 38

I will not forsake a commitment to a church body, even when it is hard.

*And let us not neglect our meeting together,*
*as some people do but encourage one another,*
*especially now that the day of his return is drawing near.*
HEBREWS 10:25

# *Connect*

Father God, You are truly relational, which is so clearly reflected in the fullness of the Godhead. As the Father, Son, and Holy Spirit, You draw us into a relationship with You. By faith in Your son, Jesus, and the working of the Holy Spirit, we have the privilege of becoming Your children and enjoying an inheritance reserved for those in Your family.

Yet, God, family is hard, whether it is by blood or by adoption or by being graphed into Your body.

---

**It seems to be our nature to desire self-sufficiency and independence, yet by Your design, we really do need one another.**

---

Help us, Lord, to be vulnerable, humble, compassionate, and sincere with one another.

Help us, Lord, to be full of grace, mercy, and forgiveness with each other.

God, give us a desire for unity in community.

Give us the ability to persevere in the family of God and embrace a commitment to fellowship, even when it is hard.

In the strong name of Jesus, Amen.

# *Consider*

When you hear the word "community," what's the first thought that comes to mind? Do you recall that time your freezer was overstocked with casseroles after walking through that dark season? Do you see in your mind's eye a gathering of friends to celebrate your birthday or the birth of your child? Or is there a total blank, because you feel like you've not actually tasted community in the context as God designed it to be?

Through those eighteen years living at a boarding school with my husband, I came to realize that the beauty of a God-orchestrated community comes from doing life together around the clock. It was in our daily meals shared in the dining hall and chit-chat afterward that cultivated connection. It was in watching one another's kiddos in a pinch and gathering together over school breaks for a potluck meal that forged friends-like-family relationships. But ultimately, it was serving one another in sickness and health, in blessings and trials, in which our connections became friendships, and our friendships became community.

See, the thing about community is that it has to be accessible in both the good times and bad to prove itself authentic and give us a sense of belonging.

*Real community happens when we show up to clean house and do laundry for a sister-in-Christ recovering from surgery.*

*Real community happens when we make time to connect with a small group of sisters-in-Christ and get honest about our struggles.*

*Real community happens when we show up wherever and whenever the family of God gathers together, even when we don't feel*

*like it ... even when it's not what we expected ... even when there
is more of us needed than we want to give.*

---

## When we make the time to invest
## in one another, we cultivate a community
## of belonging and kingdom purpose.

---

That kind of real community may be found outside of a church,
but it doesn't replace what God intends for the church.

I know that might not sit well with you. Maybe you've been one of
the wounded, as I've heard too many horror stories of sin destroying
relationships within a church community. I've experienced my own
fair share of brokenness within the family of God—even at that boarding school and in the churches I've attended since coming to know
Jesus in college.

Church sometimes hurts too much to want to enter through the
doors again.

But I also know that by not entering we're potentially not engaging with the body of Christ. And when we're not engaging, we're
missing out on a blessing that comes from God's design for provision
for community and fellowship within His family. I'm not saying we
should go back to the broken places and grasp for remnants of what
once was. But I am saying we ought to seek God for healing and try
again in a new church body.

He wants us connected, even if it is messy and scary. We don't
need to stay in dysfunction or endure abuse. Not at all! But we ought
to pursue God for His healing, His leading, and His purposes for us
within the body of Christ. Because if He calls us to it, He's got a purpose for it.

*Cultivate*

How can you make a commitment to show up, to be a part of a community of imperfect Christians, and strive together for unity and encouragement simply by doing life together?

# 39

I will use my gifts to serve the body
of Christ for the glory of God.

*There are different kinds of spiritual gifts, but the same Spirit*
*is the source of them all. There are different kinds of service,*
*but we serve the same Lord. God works in different ways,*
*but it is the same God who does the work in all of us.*
1 CORINTHIANS 12:4-6

*In his grace, God has given us different*
*gifts for doing certain things well.*
ROMANS 12:6

# Connect

God, thank you so much for making us all different and choosing to use our uniqueness in Your kingdom work.

---

**We are not replaceable. We are needed.**
**We are valuable. We have a purpose.**

---

Please forgive us when we doubt Your design and intention for our lives!

God, please prompt us to seek You more intentionally, with an open heart and mind toward discovering how You want to use our giftings in the body of Christ and as a testimony for Your glory.

Enable us to move past insecurity and comparison.

God, help us to get comfortable in our own skin and join You in Your purposes daily.

In the strong name of Jesus, Amen.

## Consider

How familiar are you with your spiritual giftings and the way God wants to use them in your life? Have you seen evidence of your giftings being used at work or in ministry, within your family or friendships?

---

**Sometimes the best way to discover our spiritual gifting is simply to be put in a situation that isn't familiar.**

---

I know that might sound strange, but it's when we are out of our comfort zone that we'll see what our natural response, God-given abilities, and spiritual giftings are. But what if you get into that situation that you're not made for? What if you completely fumble and fail? Well, it won't feel good, but it will provide you with three awesome options:

*You can depend all the more on God's power to manifest Himself through you in light of your weakness.*

*You can lean on those around you to step in and serve in their strengths, which will be a beautiful confirmation of their giftings.*

*You can walk away certain that the next time that opportunity comes up, it would be better to let someone else take on the responsibility and/or be more prepared to serve because your past experience has prepared you for such a time as this.*

This may not exactly be the course we'd like to take to figure out our spiritual gifts, but wouldn't you agree that it is all too common for us? For example, it took serving on a women's ministry team for me to discover that while I can carry out administrative tasks, my gifting is more on the side of teaching. Discussing sugar-covered cranberry recipes for the Christmas tea made me want to poke my eyes out. But I could have spent hours talking about the message and unpacking how we were going to impart the biblical application points.

Of course, another way to pinpoint your spiritual gifting is to complete a free online assessment and then prayerfully consider how the results resonate with the way you see yourself and the opportunities God places before you.

The results from gifts assessments may confirm what you feel like God has already impressed upon your heart about your spiritual gifts and spur you on to say YES to the opportunities He places before you.

You may also find a good deal of understanding as to why certain roles are hard for you to fulfill. For example, my top three spiritual gifts are discernment, teaching, and wisdom, while my bottom three are serving, giving, and mercy. Ironically, I feel like I'm surrounded by those who are richly blessed with a heart for serving and giving and mercy. When I am with them, I can often feel like, *What on earth is wrong with me? Why don't I feel that kind of generosity? Why don't I jump up to serve with a contended and willing heart?*

Well, I'm just not wired by God that way. And yet, I'm learning from these dear souls. I'm asking God to increase my heart of generosity and willingness to serve, as I take on roles that are outside of my gifting, knowing that the stretching is good for me and keeps me in a moldable place before the Lord.

The beauty is that we can learn from each other.

We can ask God to stretch us and change us. It's not that we want what others have, but that we want to be willing to be used any way God sees fit. And that we want to learn what life is like outside of our own gifting, so that He may grow within us a heart of compassion and humility, thoughtfulness and kindness. That's why we ought to embrace His sanctification and transformational work in our lives, even in the area of spiritual giftings. Because in the process of being stretched, God will deepen our giftings for His glory.

Yes, God marvelously wired us to use a particular set of gifts in His grand purposes. But that doesn't preclude Him from wanting to do even more in us, for us, and through us, all for accomplishing His Kingdom purposes.

## Cultivate

How might God want to use your giftings in your community, family, and church body? And how might He want to stretch you by growing skills and appreciation of giftings that are different from yours?

# 40

I will allow God's power to be
made perfect in my weaknesses.

*But he said to me, "My grace is sufficient for you,*
*for my power is made perfect in weakness."*
*Therefore I will boast all the more gladly about my*
*weaknesses, so that Christ's power may rest on me.*
2 CORINTHIANS 12:9

# *Connect*

God, thank you that Your grace is sufficient for us. Thank you for perfecting Your power in our weakness. God, forgive us when we run from our weaknesses. Forgive us when we hide our weakness, striving to be perfect in our own strength.

Lord, may we gladly boast in our weaknesses, as we invite You into our hearts, minds, and lives to accomplish Your purposes through Your power and strength.

---

## May Christ's power rest on us completely.

---

May nothing, not even our own attempts at being self-sufficient and independent, get in the way of that gift.

In the strong name of Jesus, Amen.

# Consider

Have you recently thought to yourself, "I was not made to do this!"?

So often we think of our weaknesses as a negative. We focus on the lack of knowledge, skill, talent, or experience. We feel shame about the way we are wired, focusing only on the negative side of our personality, temperament, and abilities.

What if our "lack of" is an opportunity for God to show up and display His glory?

God's power is absolutely ready to manifest in our weaknesses. The problem is that we don't want to let Him in. We want to be independent and self-sufficient. But why? That's not how God designed us. He created us to depend upon His power working through us, so that His strength may be seen in us.

---

## Our weakness is the key that unlocks the door to God's power.

---

I suppose I wouldn't believe this is really the way God works, except that I've had to depend on the Lord to work through my greatest weakness … my own personality and temperament. My moods swing wide and loud. My mom used to say that I was born angry. The truth is, I was born strong and fierce, passionate and driven, focused and determined, and highly observant with a long time frame orientation, and a by-product of that kind of emotional intensity is also a propensity to anger, to being driven, to wanting to be in control. How do I know all this? Well, through a whole lot of self-awareness, counseling, coaching, and insights from the Highlands Ability Battery.

This time devoted to understanding my God-given wiring has completely opened my eyes to see the beauty of His work in me and through me in both my weaknesses and strengths.

I'm a whole package. So are you. We can't throw out our weaknesses without also dismissing our strengths. Instead, we need to figure out how to yield our weaknesses to God so that He can work in them and through them.

By the grace of God, He's shown me that if my emotions and priorities are left unchecked and unyielded to Him, I will be a hot mess and disaster to live with. But when I choose to operate in submission to God with my strengths, and in honest evaluation of my weaknesses, it's a beautiful thing! Yes, I have to work at keeping my tongue bridled and heart in check. This is a daily act of dying to myself as I strive toward being kind, thoughtful, and loving. I know you might not think so, but this is my struggle and constant prayer before the Lord. There are days in which I don't do it well at all, and yet God's grace is sufficient, not only for me but also my family. My husband and children don't think any less of me for this area of weakness. They come alongside me with both encouragement and accountability, grace and truth.

When my weakness is overwhelming, it's an invitation to step into the power of God's great strength … to give Him my weakness again, so that He can be strong in me and through me.

When we are wholly yielded to the Lord in our weakness, we get to experience and witness the power of His strength at work in us.

Yes, when we are weak, He is strong.

Not quite the fair trade, but isn't that just like God?

He is generous with His sufficiency in the face of our insufficiency. Maybe it's time for you to experience this gift as you yield your weakness to Him too.

## *Cultivate*

How is your area of weakness—whether in skill, knowledge, or temperament—an opportunity for God to show His power at work in you?

# 41

I will make the most of every
opportunity the Lord gives me.

*Be very careful, then, how you live—not as
unwise but as wise, making the most of
every opportunity, because the days are evil.*
EPHESIANS 5:15-16 NIV

# Connect

God, thank you for the time You've given us.

Thank you for the reminder in Your Word that we need to be thoughtful and intentional in how we use our time.

Even on an ordinary day, when the evil in this world isn't the top news headline, we need to be so cognizant that today is indeed a gift from You.

---

## God, may we use our time wisely.

---

May our time be devoted to You.

May we yield our wants and desires unto Your plans as we embrace the opportunities You set before us.

In the strong name of Jesus, Amen.

# Consider

Paul's instruction to the Ephesians to make the most of every opportunity is as much for us today as it was on the day he wrote it. He describes the "days as evil," urging intentionality about how they were living.

*To be wise and not fools.*
*To not act thoughtlessly.*
*To understand what the Lord wants and do it.*

But how do we really know what God wants of us? Some of it is so plain …

*Live with love.*
*Follow Christ's example.*
*Be sacrificial and a pleasing aroma.*
*Be thankful unto God.*

Some of it makes us uncomfortable, fearing it's a "little judgy" …

*Don't allow sexual immorality to be among us.*
*No greed.*
*No obscene stories.*
*Nor foolish talk and coarse jokes.*
*No idolatry … no worship of the things of this world.*

Some of it sounds so beautifully poetic, but also out of reach for our sin-stained lives …

*Don't excuse sin.*
*Don't disobey God.*

*Don't participate in acts of the darkness.*
*Live as people of the light.*
*Take no part in worthless deeds of evil and darkness, instead expose them.*
*Don't be drunk on wine.*
*Be filled with the Holy Spirit.*
*Sing psalms, hymns, and spiritual songs.*
*And give thanks to God for everything in the name of Jesus.*

We might long to say, "Yes, Lord!" Yet when it comes to carrying out this command, what do our actions tell about the sincerity of our heart? When it comes to making the most of every opportunity, are we going about the business God has given us in such a way that we are the aroma of Christ and people of the light? Or are we entrapped by sin? Tempted by the deeds of darkness?

---

**What stronghold do we need to crush,**
**by the power of the Holy Spirit,**
**as we choose to live for Christ?**

---

And by doing so, how could we become His agent of hope and change, peace and purpose in every situation that He opens a door of opportunity to?

## Cultivate

How are you making the most of every opportunity God provides for you to be His hands and feet and heart and mouthpiece?

# 42

I will seek God to fill me with all joy and peace as I trust in Him that I may overflow with hope onto others by the power of the Holy Spirit at work in me.

*I pray that God, the source of hope,*
*will fill you completely with joy*
*and peace because you trust in him.*
*Then you will overflow with confident hope*
*through the power of the Holy Spirit.*
ROMANS 15:13 NIV

## Connect

God, I pray that You, the source of our hope, will fill us completely with all joy and peace as we trust in You.

---

**Please, Lord, fill us with
confident hope through the power
of the Holy Spirit at work in us.**

---

May we overflow more of You, and less of ourselves, onto our families and friends, in our workplaces and ministries, and throughout our neighborhoods and communities in which You've called us into for Your glory and good purposes.

In the strong name of Jesus, Amen.

# *Consider*

What would you say is filling you up day in and day out? What's taking up residence in your heart? What is consuming your thought-life? How are you spending your time and resources?

On an ordinary Monday, how do you find the energy to press on? When Wednesday hits, do you feel sapped of all desire to keep on going through "hump day?" What are you doing to make it to the finish line on Friday?

Maybe the promise of the weekend is your motivator. Do you bribe yourself with rewards, like a glass of wine or bowl of ice cream after dinner? Or a shopping trip, night out with the girls, or a Netflix binge?

We each crave a kind of fuel to get us through the daily grind.

And yet, I'm discovering through so many heart-honest conversations that the most God-loving, church-going, Bible-study attending women I know are secretly neglecting this awesome gift of soul-strength that God offers each one of us. Is this your struggle too?

I'm starting to call it the "great dupe."

Satan's lies are so convincing as he twists a good into a god. Like making self-motivation greater than Spirit-led living in order to endure the mundane. Or turning the pursuit of time-management techniques into the answer rather than devoting time to be with the Lord and in the Word. Planning is not wrong, but surrender at the starting point is a much better approach.

---

## God promises to fill us up with an overflowing hope that results in joy and peace.

---

But will we receive it? Will we embrace the kind of hope, joy, and peace that God offers, which is exactly what we need to get through the grind?

Like an empty glass, we can't fill ourselves.

We need the source of life to quench our souls … Jesus, Himself.

We need the filling that comes through the work of the Holy Spirit as we devote time to being in the Word each and every day—without ongoing excuses but with much overflowing grace.

So, will we become women who slow down long enough each day to be filled up to overflowing by God Himself? Will we embrace the joy and peace that comes from Him? Will we allow His hope to overflow onto our family and friends, workplaces and ministries, communities and neighbors?

Imagine that kind of transformed living. Imagine that kind of impact.

## Cultivate

What will you do to make changes in your routine so that you can be filled up by God each day?

# 43

## I will yield my financial resources to the Lord's work.

*"Bring all the tithes into the storehouse so there will be enough food in my Temple. If you do," says the Lord of Heaven's Armies, "I will open the windows of heaven for you. I will pour out a blessing so great you won't have enough room to take it in! Try it! Put me to the test!"*
MALACHI 3:10

*Jesus sat down near the collection box in the Temple and watched as the crowds dropped in their money. Many rich people put in large amounts. Then a poor widow came and dropped in two small coins. Jesus called his disciples to him and said, "I tell you the truth, this poor widow has given more than all the others who are making contributions. For they gave a tiny part of their surplus, but she, poor as she is, has given everything she had to live on."*
MARK 12:41-44

# Connect

God, You ask us to give back to You whatever You've already given to us.

Forgive us when we resist. Forgive us for holding on tightly to our finances.

When we are afraid to be generous, I ask that You would be our source of truth, perspective, and provision right where we are today.

---

## Break us from the strongholds of fear and greed.

---

God, give us a spirit of generosity and a desire for Your kingdom purposes to prevail.

Lord, may we be like the widow and not think twice about giving You everything we have to live on.

God, increase our faith and trust in You to pray this prayer with sincerity of heart.

In the strong name of Jesus, Amen.

# *Consider*

When it comes to money are you a saver or spender? Are you a budget tracker, or do you toss the receipts in the recycling bin? Do you worry about having enough money, or do you live like it is growing on trees? Is it easy for you to be generous, or do you struggle to give to those in need and tithe the full 10 percent of your income?

When you think of the way you approach your finances, can you pinpoint the way your habits were shaped? Did you inherit a philosophy by what you were taught or by what you caught?

I know this matter of finances might not seem like that big of a deal in light of choosing to live brave for the glory of God, but it is as foundational as every other principle we've considered because of what God has to say about money. He addresses generosity, stewardship, and tithing throughout the Old and New Testaments.

---

## Money matters to God, and because of that, it ought to matter to us.

---

But the problem is that our approach to money is more likely shaped by our upbringing and generational experience than it is by the principles of God's Word.

Taking the Financial Peace University course produced and taught by Dave Ramsey helped me to pinpoint my own habits and philosophy regarding money, along with providing a framework for making practical changes in my spending and saving. However, it was through an alarming and staggeringly true article that my husband shared with me that I found the missing puzzle piece in regards to my fears and habits.

I struggle with the fear of never having enough money because that was the mantra pumped into my adolescent brain.

As a Gen Xer and child of divorce, stability and money have not gone hand in hand. When I was growing up, all I remember my dad saying was that "he hadn't yet received the commission check"; meanwhile my mom would come home with clothes from the Gap for me and my sister. We seemed to never have enough money, but we didn't lack the best brands or opportunities or vacations. Turns out my parents were racking up credit card debt that I only learned about a few years ago.

Now that I'm running my own business, I understand my father's response to me every time I asked for something. The beginning of the month is frightening. The end of the month, in most cases, allows me to breathe easy … at least just enough to know that we'll be able to pay the bills.

I've been at this long enough to know the pattern, but not stop the crazy cycle of fear. In my own reasoning, I won't ever be able to because God doesn't ask me to reason … He asks me to trust Him. He requires us to look back at His faithfulness and forward at the promise of eternity while navigating the here and now.

But that is so hard to do! Some days that dance of trust takes on a beautiful rhythm. Others days, I look like I'm doing kick-boxing in a ballet class. Not so pretty!

I wonder, however, if the widow found her rhythm?

We romanticize it and think she sashayed up to the offering plate and gracefully deposited all she had. But what if she went up there kicking and screaming? What if she was bartering with God? I believe that when Jesus praised her, it was because of her obedience. I'd like to think her countenance was equally stunning. But maybe, just maybe, her trust looked as messy as mine and yours as she yielded her heart to the One she ultimately knew was her provider.

What is your financial story? How is God about the business of transforming you in regards to how you spend, save, and give for His glory?

# 44

I will seek justice, love mercy,
and walk humbly all of my days.

*He has shown you, O mortal, what is good.*
*And what does the Lord require of you?*
*To act justly and to love mercy*
*and to walk humbly with your God.*
MICAH 6:8 NIV

# Connect

Thank you for giving us such simple and clear instructions in Your Word. Really, all we have to do is say yes to You.

---

## Our responsibility is simply to put Your Word into action.

---

And yet, as simple as that sounds, how difficult it is for us as our flesh and mind battle against the Spirit and truth.

Lord, we ask You for an infusion of Your presence and a conviction of Your truth so that we may do what You require of us ... to act justly, love mercy, and walk humbly with You.

Yes, Lord, may we walk in the strength and power You provide through Jesus Christ and the working of the Holy Spirit so that we can fulfill Your purposes.

In the strong name of Jesus, Amen.

# *Consider*

Seek Justice. Love Mercy. Walk Humbly.

How often do we see these words imprinted on a T-shirt, journal, or an eye-catching social media graphic? It's such a perfect little ditty, a great slogan, that we might think that God was really the first to launch a marketing campaign. Yet, God's Word was never meant to be used for feel-good sound bites. It's meant to be read, reflected upon, and applied.

So let's go there. Let's think about what these words really mean in our everyday lives.

*What are we doing to seek justice?*

How do we seek justice as a home-keeper or school teacher? A writer or ministry leader? A mom or a friend? Do we have to become a lawyer or serve with the International Justice Mission? Do we have to be a missionary in an oppressed country? Or is justice something we can seek out right where God has already planted us while also prayerfully and financially supporting those who are reaching beyond our walls to fight for justice for all human beings?

*What are we doing to fulfill the call to love mercy?*

If we love mercy, how does that manifest itself in our lives? Does it change the way we respond to offenses? Is it evident in the words we use to speak of others? Is it visible by our actions? Is it seen in our choice to serve instead of being served, even if the one receiving our sacrifice "isn't worth it" from our human perspective?

*What does it look like to walk humbly with our God?*

How do we walk humbly with God when we can't even see God? Is this call about walking in such a way that we're continually aware of God's presence and yielded to His purposes? Does this play out in our family relationships? Our workplace? In public social settings? If being humble is not about low self-worth, but rather thinking of others in light of the cross, then how are we fulfilling this call? Are we following Christ's example in the way He walked humbly in obedience to His Father on our behalf (Philippians 2)?

---

## If we're going to call ourselves Christians, shouldn't we walk the walk and talk the talk that reflects the heart of God and His purposes?

---

It may not be easy. It certainly will be messy. But if we yield our flesh to the Spirit's leading, I'm pretty certain that our Father in heaven, through the power of Christ at work in our lives, will show us exactly how to seek justice, love mercy, and walk humbly with our God.

*Cultivate*

What is your perspective on this call from God to seek justice, love mercy, and walk humbly with Him?

# 45

I will defend the cause of the
fatherless, the poor, the oppressed.

*Defend the weak and the fatherless;*
*uphold the cause of the poor and the oppressed.*
PSALM 82:3 NIV

# Connect

God, please make us sensitive to the needs of those around us, especially the fatherless, the poor, and the oppressed.

Please keep us from being numb and living desensitized to the struggles of those around us.

Keep us from turning our backs on those who are weak.

Motivate us to lend a helping hand and be Your ambassadors in the flesh.

---

**Open our eyes to seek the emotionally, spiritually, and physically orphaned among us and look for ways to respond to their needs with Your love as our driving force.**

---

Give us a fire in our souls for upholding the cause of the poor and oppressed.

God, may we be Your hands and feet to every single person You allow us to come in contact with each and every day.

In the strong name of Jesus, Amen.

# Consider

Could it be that we hesitate to read and apply God's Word because we're afraid we simply won't measure up?

What if we haven't defended the weak and the fatherless? What if we don't uphold the cause of the poor and the oppressed?

Or, what if we have, but it looks different than what the world defines as social justice, mercy projects, and orphan care?

When I consider what it looks like to defend the weak and fatherless, uphold the cause of the poor and oppressed, one clear image comes to mind. It's like a word bubble of all the organizations devoted to fulfilling this kind of mission.

As you dig into the backstory, most of these organizations began organically … inspired by an experience and challenged by a need. For example, the Akola Project and Project Nyamensa were started by privileged girls whose eyes were opened to the suffering of women an ocean away. I once knew these girls … as ordinary high school students wondering if they would make a difference in this world. No doubt they have, and honestly, I couldn't be more proud. But what about the rest of their classmates? What about the men and women who poured their lives into them in unseen ways?

Do we have to start something big for it to mean something to God?

Is giving money or volunteering for these organizations enough?

Is it okay to simply be an advocate but not a visionary-doer when it comes to meeting the needs of the fatherless, the needy, the poor, the oppressed?

Or maybe, fulfilling this call will come in a form that is so small, we may not even realize that we're doing it.

When we took in our spiritually adopted daughter, my husband and I didn't stop and say, "Wait, does this fulfill a biblical command?" Nope. We just did it. We saw a need and responded, even before we reached the point of trusting God for the next step. She became "ours" only because we were allowing the Spirit to lead instead of being waylaid by the flesh. Trust me, there were plenty of times in the ensuing years that the flesh was challenged. Praise God, His work won out!

---

**God's call for us to care for those in need isn't a "when" or "where" or even "how" question. It's actually really a "what" question … "What will you do when the need arises?"**

---

What will you do when the opportunity presents itself?

What will you do to be sensitive to the needs of those around you?

What will you do to be the hands and feet of God in action to a world that desperately needs both His touch and His love?

## Cultivate

How is God prompting you to prepare and respond to the needs of the weak and fatherless, the poor and oppressed?

# 46

I will speak the Good News and live out the Gospel in private and public.

*I do not hide your righteousness in my heart;*
*I speak of your faithfulness and your saving help.*
*I do not conceal your love and your*
*faithfulness from the great assembly.*
PSALM 40:10 NIV

*And this gospel of the kingdom will be*
*preached in the whole world as a testimony*
*to all nations, and then the end will come.*
MATTHEW 24:14 NIV

# *Connect*

God, we don't want to hide Your righteousness in our hearts because we want to be women who speak of Your faithfulness and saving help. May we not ever conceal Your love or faithfulness from those who desperately need to know You and embrace You for themselves.

---

**Please give us the courage to speak
of the Gospel message to every listening ear.**

---

May this be a part of our kingdom mission. May we preach Your Good News to the whole world, to be a testimony to all nations before the end comes.

In the strong name of Jesus, Amen.

# *Consider*

What does it look like for you to speak the Good News and live it out in your personal and private life? Maybe you think of the misquote attributed to Francis Assisi, "Preach the Gospel, and if necessary, use words." Yes, The Gospel Coalition website published a report that the monk didn't actually say those words, which is actually a good thing because the principle isn't even biblically sound.

Throughout Scripture we find the call to go forth and preach the Good News. It's plain. It's simple. And it comes straight from Jesus. "He said to them, 'Go into all the world and preach the gospel to all creation'" (Mark 16:15 NLT).

Make no mistake, "preach" means exactly what you think it does … to speak aloud:

- to proclaim after the manner of a herald
- to publish, proclaim openly: something which has been done
- used of the public proclamation of the gospel and matters pertaining to it, made by John the Baptist, by Jesus, by the apostles and other Christian teachers[1]

Preach is what our preachers do on Sunday mornings and weekday podcasts. But it is also what we, as followers of Christ, have been commissioned to do in everyday relationships and ordinary conversations.

---

**Where our hearts are connected to others, we're called to pour forth the Words of God and His very good news.**

---

It doesn't have to be eloquent or steeped in theological jargon. Actually, it's probably better if we use our natural vernacular and even

---

1 Source: https://www.blueletterbible.org/lang/lexicon/lexicon.cfm?Strongs=G2784&t=NLT)

throw in a bit of our most common slang. It won't necessarily be easy to find the words to express the Good News. The same urging Paul offered Timothy likely applies to us. We will have to "work at telling others the Good News" in order to fully carry out this ministry God has given to us.

*But you should keep a clear mind in every situation. Don't be afraid of suffering for the Lord. Work at telling others the Good News, and fully carry out the ministry God has given you.*

2 TIMOTHY 4:5

In the face of our own insecurities, we can cling to this truth: Our life's greatest mission is to be used in God's kingdom work of bringing the Good News to every nation, starting with the very people He's put us in relationship with. But in order to do so effectively, we need to live it out authentically.

We need to dig into the Word daily.

We need to sit with the Lord and invite the Holy Spirit to bring the Scriptures alive in our hearts and minds.

We need to be willing to think biblically in a world that will challenge us to pursue emotional relevancy and comfort.

We need to act on the Word in every way, demonstrating our love of the Lord through our obedience to His commands.

We can't be ambassadors of the Good News if our hearts and minds are not connected with the God we represent.

## Cultivate

What will it take for you to authentically live out the Scriptures so that you can confidently be a messenger of the Good News?

# 47

I will accept the trouble and
suffering that comes into my life,
knowing that God will equip me
to endure and be my comforter.

*Therefore do not worry about tomorrow, for tomorrow will
worry about itself. Each day has enough trouble of its own.*
MATTHEW 6:34 NIV

*We can rejoice, too, when we run into problems and
trials, for we know that they help us develop endurance.*
ROMANS 5:3

*And our hope for you is firm, because we know that just as
you share in our sufferings, so also you share in our comfort.*
2 CORINTHIANS 1:7 NIV

# Connect

God, do You tell us to not worry about tomorrow, because You know we will worry about tomorrow?

Is that because we desire order? Because we thrive when we have a plan and sense of purpose? Or is it because You designed us for eternity and we ache for it in this world of trouble?

We suffer in this fallen place … our temporary home. We long for a time when there will be no more tears, no more sorrow, no more death. But for now, we have to endure the suffering that will come.

You say that we can rejoice in these trials because they develop endurance in us. Oh, but Lord, that isn't easy for us to do. We put too much stock in our circumstances instead of putting our hope in You.

God, help us to keep our minds focused on You instead of the false "comforts" of this world that tell us we deserve the "easy" life.

---

## Lord, turn our mind afresh to Your promises.

---

May we remember that as we suffer, You share in our sufferings.

In knowing our suffering, You can and always will be our source of comfort.

In the strong name of Jesus, Amen.

# *Consider*

Would you describe yourself as someone who suffers well? Do you face trials with poise and grace? Or does even the mention of suffering turn you into a hot mess?

While I had been through difficult times in my life, I never really categorized any of those hardships as suffering until this one life-changing moment on a Wednesday evening smack in the middle of summer. We were away at a Christian family camp, sitting under the teaching of James MacDonald. He spent the whole week preaching on the topic of suffering, and until that Wednesday evening session, I didn't think it really applied to me. It didn't matter that he said, "Everyone is either in the middle of a trial, coming out of a trial, or about to go back into one." For some reason, I thought I didn't fit the mold.

Until that night.

---

**When I finally realized that I was in the middle of a trial that was so long it simply felt normal.**

---

Can you relate? Is the suffering you're experiencing more like years rather than just a season passing by?

At that time, I was two years into a falling out with my dad. Two years of wondering if I'd ever see him again. Two years recounting the hurtful words, lies, and accusations. Two years grieving his absence. Two years of hating Father's Day.

But for two years, I never really identified it as a trial nor considered what good God might want to accomplish in me and through me in the middle of my suffering. That's because I never really saw that I was suffering. It just was. Until I began to the connect the pieces as I listened to Pastor MacDonald. That night I was left with two questions ringing in my ears.

*Am I willing to glorify God in the middle of this trial instead of finding a way out of it?*

*Am I willing to love God and obey Him, even if He doesn't take this from me?*

Those questions pounded through my mind and heart as my eyes welled so full it felt like two years worth of tears were breaking forth. I cried for at least an hour, falling on my face before the Lord. I allowed myself to feel the pain and the loss, instead of denying it. I finally was in a place of accepting the reality of this trial.

That mid-summer night, I yielded my suffering to the Lord on the shores of the most beautiful lake.

I gave God my dad. My sorrow. My expectations.

Over the next two years, God accomplished such a healing on my heart, freeing me from the pain and enabling me to forgive my dad.

The suffering turned into full surrender, which is the only way to move through our trials.

Only when we acknowledge our trouble before God can we then place them in the hands of the One who was meant to carry them in the first place. And in that release, we find the comfort and strength to carry on.

## Cultivate

What is your current trial? How are you suffering? What does it look like to acknowledge it and give it over to the Lord?

# 48

I will always choose to believe
that God is indeed holy, kind,
loving, faithful, merciful, and just.

*Don't you see how wonderfully kind, tolerant, and patient*
*God is with you? Does this mean nothing to you? Can't you*
*see that his kindness is intended to turn you from your sin?*
ROMANS 2:4

*The faithful love of the Lord never ends! His mercies never cease.*
*Great is his faithfulness; his mercies begin afresh each morning.*
LAMENTATIONS 3:22-23

*Your love, Lord, reaches to the heavens, your faithfulness to the skies*
PSALM 36:5 NIV

# Connect

God, thank you for being so wonderfully kind, tolerant, and patient with us. May we not dismiss the way You treat us nor take it for granted. But may we embrace Your kindness and the way it calls us to turn from our sin.

---

**Your faithful love never ends, God!**
**Your mercies never cease!**
**Your great faithfulness pours out**
**on us in fresh mercies each morning.**

---

Thank you, Lord, that Your love reaches as high as the heavens but also deep into our hearts.

In the strong name of Jesus, Amen.

# Consider

What is your natural reaction when you get caught for doing something wrong? Oh, I know, maybe you're smart enough at this point in your life to avoid doing something wrong … or getting caught. But in all seriousness, can you think of a moment in which you knew you were up to no good? Headed in the wrong direction? Disobeying God's best?

I only ask because I want you to think about what God's response was in that situation and how you, in turn, responded to Him. Did you run away? Try to hide? Laugh it off? Deny it entirely? Blame someone else?

What was God's response? Did He strike you down with a thunderbolt? Ignore you for days? Scoop you up and tell you not to worry about it? Come to think of it, that sounds more like modern-day parenting techniques, minus the thunderbolt, compared to how God works.

According to Scripture, God is wonderfully kind, tolerant, and patient, but not without due cause.

---

**His kindness is intended to turn us from sin.**

---

Is that how it is working in your life? Or do you find yourself scared of God's wrath, fearful of His judgment, anxious at the potential of unleashing His anger? Actually, if we think about that side of God's character enough, it might actually motivate you to stay committed to living out His Word.

## Cultivate

How is God's character shaping and motivating you to live according to His commands? What is your response to dealing with sin in your life in light of who God is?

# 49

I will strive to lay down my life for others as Christ has done for me.

*Greater love has no one than this:*
*to lay down one's life for one's friends.*
JOHN 15:13 NIV

# Connect

God, the thought of laying down our lives for others as You have done for us is simply terrifying.

No matter how much we want to be like You and follow Your example, the reality is that the sacrifice You made for us is one we could never imagine being expected of us.

To die. On the cross. To have our blood shed for another.

You chose to be obedient to Your Father in heaven. This is the sacrifice You made for us because You love us! But could we ever be that obedient? Ever filled with that much love for a friend?

---

**Lord, please show us what it practically looks like to love others to the extent of laying down our life for them.**

---

In the strong name of Jesus, Amen.

# Consider

How often does the thought of laying down your life for someone else cross your mind? Hmm. As we carry on about our days, we may be sacrificially serving through preparing a meal, washing a load of clothes, or pouring a cup of coffee for a friend or colleague, but serving is quite different from laying down your life. Maybe for those who serve as caregivers, the thought of laying down their lives to the point of death is something much more tangible. And for those who have received an organ in order to continue living and breathing, the reality of life-for-life is entirely true.

---

**But for the vast majority of us, we don't understand this call from God to lay down our lives for a friend as Jesus commands.**

---

Until that moment of crisis comes when we come face to face with the brokenness of our earthly bodies and the preciousness of life.

When a loved one gets so sick they can't care for themselves. When what once was considered private no longer has such stigma. When living becomes harder than dying because you can no longer do it on your own.

I think in those kinds of situations we get a taste of what Christ has done for us … but only a taste.

When our friends sat across from us on our porch one early fall night, with a crisp breeze blowing through, we had no idea what storm was coming our way. They shared the cancer diagnosis, and we knew the trial was impending. But we didn't know how integral our role would be. Sure, we'd pray. Of course, we'd cook some meals and care for the kids. But nothing could prepare us for that night in the emergency room when post-surgery complications made our friend so horribly sick and weak. You just don't think about what it will be like to care for your brother-in-Christ in a way that friends don't normally do—caring for their bodies and not just their hearts.

That night I watched my husband serve. I saw his Christlikeness afresh. He moved one step closer to fulfilling the call to lay down his life for a friend, as he entered into the uncomfortable, the intimate, the necessary steps of love.

## Cultivate

In what ways is God calling you to sacrificially love to the point of laying your life down for a friend?

# 50

I will obey God because I love God.

*But if anyone obeys his word, love for God is truly*
*made complete in them. This is how we know we are in him:*
*Whoever claims to live in him must live as Jesus did.*
1 JOHN 2:5-6 NIV

# Connect

God, thank you for loving us before we could even respond in love to You. Thank you for giving us Your Word. Thank you for giving us Jesus to save us from our sins and make a way to be in a right relationship with You.

Thank you, God, for the gift of the Holy Spirit and the way You guide us and fill us with Your presence.

We want to show You our love in return, and we know that comes in the form of obeying Your Word.

---

**Please give us both the desire and necessary conviction to obey You and live according to the Scriptures.**

---

In the strong name of Jesus, Amen.

# Consider

When our kiddos were barely old enough to walk and talk, we introduced them to a little morning cheer. Holding up both our hands to give them high-fives, we shouted, "Joyfully OBEY hey!" I know it sounds corny, but it worked, especially for our less than compliant children. But there was a purpose behind our little chant.

We wanted to remind our children that obedience was an important goal they could obtain while putting a positive spin on the expectation before a disciplinary moment was required. We also wanted to emphasize that obedience should show up with its partner ... JOY.

---

## We didn't want to have kiddos who simply "knew" how to behave.

---

We wanted our little human beings to grow up into big human beings with the capability of getting their heart in the right place too because one day they would have to answer to God for both their motives and their actions.

While this little habit of chanting "joyfully obey hey" may seem like it was just a parenting tactic, it was also a daily reminder to us as parents to stay in the game—to invest the time necessary to train them up as an expression of both our love for them and for God as we stewarded their little souls.

As I look back on this critical season of life in which we were shaping their character, I can't help but think how the Lord was shaping mine. The same end goal I had for them ...

*to obey joyfully*
*to be mindful about the state of their heart*
*to be hopeful in their potential*
*to do it from an overflow of love*

… is actually the same end goal God has for us.

---

**God gave us His word to obey.**
**He gave us Jesus as an example to follow.**
**He gave us His love before**
**we ever even knew we needed it.**

---

So what will it take for us to become like little children before God and respond from the purest place of love with a desire to obey His Word joyfully?

## Cultivate

What is standing in the way of you choosing to obey God from the overflow of your love for Him?

# 51

I will put on the full armor of God
as I fight against the enemy of God
and not the people of God.

*Finally, be strong in the Lord and in his mighty power. Put on the*
*full armor of God, so that you can take your stand against the*
*devil's schemes. For our struggle is not against flesh and blood,*
*but against the rulers, against the authorities, against the powers of*
*this dark world and against the spiritual forces of evil in the heavenly*
*realms. Therefore put on the full armor of God, so that when the*
*day of evil comes, you may be able to stand your ground, and after*
*you have done everything, to stand.... And pray in the Spirit on all*
*occasions with all kinds of prayers and requests. With this in mind,*
*be alert and always keep on praying for all the Lord's people. Pray*
*also for me, that whenever I speak, words may be given me so that I*
*will fearlessly make known the mystery of the gospel ...*

EPHESIANS 6:10-19 NIV

# Connect

God, please make us strong in the Lord and Your mighty power. Give us the determination to put on the full armor You provide so that we make take our stand against the devil's schemes. God, we know that the struggle is not against flesh and blood, but against the powers of this dark world and the spiritual forces of evil in the heavenly realms.

---

**God, may we put on our full armor
so that when the day of evil comes,
we may be able to stand our
ground no matter what.**

---

Thank you, God, that You make us strong with the belt of truth buckled around our waist and the breastplate of righteousness in place. May we keep our feet fitted with the readiness that comes from the gospel of peace. May we take up our shield of faith with which we can extinguish all the flaming arrows of the evil one. May we put on the helmet of salvation and the sword of the spirit, which is the Word of God.

And may we pray in the Spirit on all occasions with all kinds of prayers and requests for Your people.

God, may we fearlessly make known the mystery of the gospel.

In the strong name of Jesus, Amen.

# *Consider*

As we were putting laundry away, I was recounting to my husband an incident that happened earlier in the day that had really knocked my confidence to the ground. The words that a woman spoke to me were clearly from a place of her own pain, but between the timing and my own tender heart, they struck me right to the core. I spent the whole day trying to preach truth to my soul.

I know how to take captive every thought and make it obedient to Christ. I know how to be transformed by the renewing of my mind.

Goodness, my whole book is based on this principle. Everything about my healing has been a result of believing that our thought life matters, and that we need to soak in the truth in the face of the lies the enemy will spin our way.

But in that moment, I was worn down and struggling to believe the truth that sets me free. And I was growing more and more irritable, rather than finding the peace I craved. Just as I was about to launch into my upteenth reason about why that woman was out of line, my son appeared in the doorway innocently munching on a PB&J sandwich. I snapped at him, "What do you want? I'm talking to dad."

Based on the look on his face and the way he scurried away, I could tell I was out of line. I turned to Stephen with a knowing look, and he confirmed it.

"Buddy," I hollered to the other room. He sheepishly returned. "Was I disrespectful in my reaction to you?"

"Yep."

"Ugh, I'm sorry. Will you forgive me?"

"Yep," he said with a tender smile.

For some reason, I thought maybe I should ask this twelve-year-old-son of mine for his perspective, so I shared with him what had happened earlier in the day.

"So, what do you think my problem is?" I asked when I was done.

"It's like what you were saying to me last week. I think you need to give it to God and remember that the battle is in the spiritual realm."

Out of the mouth of babes. He was right. I was busy fighting a battle in the flesh, within my own emotions and against another woman who would never hear my thoughts (thank goodness).

What I was really doing was fighting in a war against the enemy of God—Satan. His minions were at work undermining every ounce of God's good purposes that had been manifested in my life that morning and throughout the remainder of the day. While I was taking up the Word of God and preaching it to my own mind, I neglected to use it as a sword against the devil. It wasn't just my heart and mind that needed to take up a different battle stance.

The enemy needed to get off my territory and retreat far, far away.

---

**When God tells us to take a stand, it's only the first posture we are to assume, because that's what prepares us for every defensive and offensive move necessary to do battle against the enemy.**

---

God instructs us to put on His armor. This is not a passive move. It's not casual. It's intentional and purposeful. We are to buckle the truth around our waist, secure His righteousness across our chest, fit our feet with the gospel of peace, take up the shield of faith, put on our salvation, and arm ourselves with the Word of God.

In any and every situation, we must be prepared for battle with the prince of darkness, bathed in prayer and determined to gain the victory found in Christ as we fearlessly make known the gospel of truth.

## *Cultivate*

How is the enemy attacking you? What can you do in response, keeping in mind God's offer of His armor?

# 52

I will seek to live as a chosen, holy, dearly loved child of God who has been called out of darkness and into His wonderful light, that I may tell others about His marvelous works and praise His holy name.

*Therefore, as God's chosen people, holy and dearly loved, clothe your-selves with compassion, kindness, humility, gentleness and patience.*
COLOSSIANS 3:1 2 NIV

*But you are a chosen people, a royal priesthood, a holy nation, God's special possession, that you may declare the praises of him who called you out of darkness into his wonderful light.*
1 PETER 2:9 NIV

# Connect

God, thank you for choosing us to be Your holy and dearly loved daughters. May we walk in that identity, clothing ourselves with compassion, kindness, gentleness, and patience.

---

## Lord, help us to remember who we are and whose we are.

---

Yes, God, You have made us a chosen people, a royal priesthood, a holy nation, set apart as Your special possession. We are here to declare Your praises, because You have called us out of the darkness and into Your wonderful light.

May we always remember the purpose of this journey, pressing forward with You and for You. May we not get stuck in the past. May we live with eternity at the forefront of our minds.

In the strong name of Jesus, Amen.

# Consider

What words do you use to describe the essence of who you are? When you look in the mirror. When you remember your past. When you think of yourself in this present moment. As you think about the future.

What does your word cloud look like? Is it filled with words like ...

*chosen*
*holy*
*dearly loved*
*created in His image*
*fearfully and wonderfully made*
*gifted*
*anointed*
*masterpiece*

My guess is that the first words that came to your mind were more indicative of your failures and mistakes, shame and regrets, rather than reflecting the truth of who you are in Christ.

Maybe there's some truth in those harsh words. Maybe you did mess up and are filled with remorse. But your behavior doesn't define who you are or what God wants to accomplish through you.

---

**When Christ died on the cross for your sin, He died for all of it. Past. Present. Future.**

---

You'll never be good enough, smart enough, capable enough.

You'll never arrive at a place where you have it all together.

So what if you gave up trying to be enough and simply began being you?

What if you embraced the identity God gives you as His holy, chosen, and dearly loved child? What if you embraced His truth that you are His special possession with a divine appointment to declare to the world the good news of the One who took you out of darkness and brought you into this wonderful life of light.

What if moving forward, brave and bold, bright and beautiful, was simply about being present in the identity God has given you today?

## Cultivate

What is standing in the way of you receiving your identity in Christ and living into it every single day?

# About the Author

Elisa Pulliam is the founder of *More to Be,* a ministry devoted to helping women experience a fresh encounter with God and His Word. As a coach, speaker, writer, and creative strategist she counts it a privilege to help women live transformed, equipped, and intentional on impacting the next generation with Kingdom hope as they join in God's work for their lives.

She is the author of numerous books, including, *Meet the New You: A 21-Day Plan for Embracing Fresh Attitudes and Focused Habits for Real Life Change, Unblinded Faith: Gaining Spiritual Sight through Believing God's Word,* and *Impact Together: Biblical Mentoring Simplified.*

Elisa counts her primary ministry to her Christ-with-skin-on husband and their four teenage children. Connect with Elisa at MoretoBe. com.

# About More to Be

The ministry of *More to Be* exists to help women experience a fresh encounter with God and His Word, so that they can live transformed and impact the next generation with Kingdom hope.

Through offering one-on-one life coaching, biblical life coach training, mentor training, books, downloadable resources, online courses, and the More to Be Podcast, the team at *More to Be* equips women in all seasons and stages of life with confidence and courage to join God in His work everyday.

# Acknowledgments

I am so grateful to the Lord for the opportunity to spend my days writing about His Word and sharing the good news. Even though I've been living out the gift of my salvation for the last two decades, there's hardly a day that goes by that I don't remember what life was like before and feel a tremendous sense of gratitude for the hope I have now and promise of eternity. In Christ alone, I have found the solid ground on which I stand.

I am also incredibly grateful to husband and children and the way they continually inspire me to become more bright, more beautiful more like Jesus.

*But whenever someone turns to the Lord, the veil is taken away. For the Lord is the Spirit, and wherever the Spirit of the Lord is, there is freedom. So all of us who have had that veil removed can see and reflect the glory of the Lord. And the Lord—who is the Spirit—makes us more and more like him as we are changed into his glorious image.*

2 Corinthians 3:16-18

I'm also super thankful for Kalie Kelch and her attention to detail, thoughtful feedback, and tremendous support as she worked on this manuscript with me.

## Helping You Experience a Fresh Encounter with God and His Word

God wants to use you in a mighty way to impact and influence those around you. His calling is right beneath you, and the way He wants to use you is right where He's planted you. But maybe you're not quite sure how.

At *More to Be*, we're committed to helping you find the answer.

You'll find tools and resources to help you connect with God and study His Word through our collection of Bible studies, devotionals, and online courses, as well as life coaching, coach training, and mentor training opportunities.

*free*
RESOURCES and
SPECIALS for YOU
*visit*
MORETOBE.COM

# MORETOBE.COM

Made in the USA
Columbia, SC
27 December 2019